WHAT READERS ARE

Have you ever had a conversation w̶̶̶̶̶̶̶̶̶̶̶̶
lenged you to step out of your com̶̶̶̶̶̶̶̶̶̶̶̶
Van Buskirk! Martha has a winsome way of communicating biblical truths and practical tips that are both relevant and genuine. Her unpretentious writing style blended with well-researched information is a win for me. Enjoy the process as she inspires you to take a little risk because our community needs light and grace.

—**EDEN KEEFE,** LWML president 2023–2027

I love Martha's reminders that *every* person has value and purpose from God, no matter his or her role or life stage. Her personal stories and Scripture references help us apply the Word to our daily—and even "ordinary"—lives. . . . Great for a small group or individual study!

—**DIANE BAHN,** Texas District (LCMS) Care and Coaching Team

Ordinary Lives, Extraordinary Grace is a truly inspiring resource. Right from the start, Martha invites us to explore practical ways our ordinary lives can make a big difference by taking one divinely inspired step at a time. . . . No special skills or equipment needed—simply kindness and a willingness to help others. . . . Whether you are a lifelong Christian or are new to the faith, this book provides fresh eyes on how to live a purpose-filled life anchored in God's grace.

—**DONNA SNOW,** founder of Artesian Ministries, Christian author and speaker

"Folks . . . shine because their hearts are anchored in the Lord." That is a wonderful affirmation from Martha to encourage all of us ordinary people. She gives practical, thoughtful, and honest insights to help us really "see" others. We can serve our families, our neighbors, and even our communities with "mobile shine."

—**CONSTANCE DENNINGER,** co-founder of Visual Faith® Ministry

Martha adroitly weaves biblical wisdom with her own life journey to allow each of us to discover our unique role in being the hands and feet of God. *Ordinary Lives, Extraordinary Grace* is a perfect resource for couples and small Bible study groups who seek to individually and collectively live out the unique role God has created for each of us.

—**LAURIE AND KURT SENSKE,** spouses, parents, grandparents, servants

Gracious has become a jargonish adjective, overused and misunderstood. Martha Van Buskirk places the word *gracious* back where it belongs: rooted in God's saving acts in Jesus Christ and related to "our everyday shining spaces"; rooted in the biblical witness in order to be related to family, community, the workplace, and the challenges of real life.

—**REV. DR. JOHN ARTHUR NUNES**, interim president, California Lutheran University

The beauty of this book is that it takes all the differences that separate us and boils them down to one simple truth: people need Jesus. We are all valuable souls created by God, and God uses ordinary people to share His extraordinary grace. . . . With obvious enthusiasm, Martha encourages readers to take a step in faith, follow the Holy Spirit's nudging, and get out of their comfort zones to let their light shine!

—**RUTH MEYER**, author of *Our Faith from A to Z*, *Grace Alone*, and *N is for Nativity*

While we may see ourselves as ordinary, God always sees us with a higher purpose. Martha is clear that the Holy Spirit, working through Word and Sacrament, enables us in our Christian walk. Her insight into Scripture is truly astounding as she weaves God's Word to empower and encourage us to be the light of Christ where we are.

—**PASTOR WAYNE AND KATHY GRAUMANN**, Montgomery, Texas

Martha's generous hospitality and ability to shine the light in the every day are not a shiny facade. These qualities are the real deal, the light of Christ shining through her. In this book, Martha gives a glimpse into how sharing Jesus with others through everyday moments is exactly the lift our world so desperately needs.

—**REV. MARK AND LAURA PULLIAM**, pastor and director of Christian education, Lazarus Church, Spring, Texas

Often, many of us feel inadequate . . . to share our faith in Jesus. This book provides an easy-to-read, Scripture-based explanation of how we can share our love for Jesus with family, friends, and even strangers we meet throughout our ordinary lives.

—**URSULA SOHNS,** pastor's wife and retired college English professor

Martha asks, "How can I shine this light [the Gospel] more graciously and generously in my home, neighborhood, and daily journey?" . . . Martha helps us see how even the ordinary settings of life can be places for God's grace to shine brightly.

—**REV. DR. DAVID BAHN**, congregation support specialist

ORDINARY Lives, EXTRAORDINARY Grace

GOD'S PURPOSE IN YOUR EVERY DAY

Martha Van Buskirk

CONCORDIA PUBLISHING HOUSE • SAINT LOUIS

To my dear family, with love.

Published by Concordia Publishing House
3558 S. Jefferson Ave., St. Louis, MO 63118–3968
1-800-325-3040 • cph.org

Manufactured in the United States of America

1 2 3 4 5 6 7 8 9 10   33 32 31 30 29 28 27 26 25 24

CONTENTS

INTRODUCTION

Have you ever had that experience when one person, one moment, one conversation or gesture or encouragement—though it was just a small thing—made all the difference in the world to you? A smile or a kind word. A listening ear or a thoughtful response. A meal or a ride to the doctor. A hug and a prayer, right in the moment. Real, specific action that caused you to feel heartened, grateful, and maybe even closer to your heavenly Father.

These small but important kindnesses can be done by anyone, but when they are done by Christians as a joyful response to the gifts and salvation that Christ has given, then they reflect the light that Jesus shines on the world. Shining for Jesus lifts the heart of the doer and the recipient. Consider "This Little Light of Mine," a spiritual and favorite song for generations. Often sung as part of ministry to children, this lively tune is an encouragement for believers of all ages. The joy-filled, inspirational theme speaks to each of us:

This little light of mine, I'm gonna let it shine;
This little light of mine, I'm gonna let it shine;
This little light of mine, I'm gonna let it shine,
Let it shine, let it shine, let it shine.

Ev'rywhere I go, I'm gonna let it shine;
Ev'rywhere I go, I'm gonna let it shine;
Ev'rywhere I go, I'm gonna let it shine,
Let it shine, let it shine, let it shine.

Jesus gave it to me, I'm gonna let it shine;
Jesus gave it to me, I'm gonna let it shine;
Jesus gave it to me, I'm gonna let it shine,
Let it shine, let it shine, let it shine.[1]

Perhaps you have sung the chorus as "This little Gospel light of mine," or you have sung other verses such as "All around my neighborhood" and "Don't let Satan blow it out." Each adaptation inspires our witness, action, and perseverance. Each stanza encourages us to hold fast to faith, living it out and walking it out everywhere we go in everything we do, as best we can, and to be witnesses of this light:

And the Word became flesh and dwelt among us, and we have seen His glory, glory as of the only Son from the Father, full of grace and truth. (John 1:14)

During the COVID-19 pandemic, many of us took time to reflect on our personal place and situation. Important and devastating things also happened during those years, adding to the world's suffering and unrest. Hope and heartening seemed to have left the world and our own lives.

That was when I got to thinking about my own ministry. What impact could I have, if any, with my one little life? How could God use me, work through me, inspire me, and guide me for His good purposes?

But you are a chosen race, a royal priesthood, a holy nation, a people for His own possession, that you may proclaim the excellencies of Him who called you out of darkness into His marvelous light. (1 Peter 2:9)

---

1   The legendary Horace Clarence Boyer (1935–2009), a foremost scholar in African American gospel music, arranged a setting for these traditional words, which is included in *One and All Rejoice* (St. Louis: Concordia Publishing House, 2020), 306.

My husband is a pastor. My father, grandfather, and two great-grandfathers were pastors. All were graduates of the same seminary. Each one's calling, faith, and life work are inspirations to me. Their wives—my mom, grandmother, and great-grandmothers—lived lovingly alongside as spiritual partners, faithfully serving the Lord and shining in their own unique settings and circumstances. Certainly, my family members who served God in this hands-on way impacted people with their example and teaching.

But I wondered: Where do I fit in?

Socially, I'm often awkward, sometimes not saying anything but other times saying too much. Sometimes I don't help, but other times I try to help too much. In true "Martha" fashion, every now and then I get stuck in the world's distractions and fail to focus on what's most important. Yet I struggle along—led and encouraged by the Holy Spirit—toward increasing alignment with God's good purposes for my life.

What I need is light, and Jesus offers this light. He says, "I am the light of the world. Whoever follows Me will not walk in darkness, but will have the light of life" (John 8:12).

I need this light of Jesus every day in my own heart to remind me of His saving grace, to keep me secure, and to guide my way. This light—His light—shines in me and through me so others might be blessed by Him.

Through my time in God's Word, the Holy Spirit began to lead and show me the incredible power of His love and kindness in a new way, combined with seeing—really seeing—those around me. This awareness provided a new way of noticing and attending to nudges from the Spirit: that even the small helps to others in our day-to-day lives are significant to God, lovely reflections of our faith, and door-openers to people in need.

The joy of the LORD** is my strength.** (Nehemiah 8:10)

I was inspired by this thought: How can I shine this light more graciously and generously in my home, neighborhood, and daily journey? To shine beyond myself, to take that next step to those around me, to move within and beyond my cozy home and beloved church?

This book flows from the inspiration of what can happen when God gives us fresh eyes (and ears) for others. What marvelous things Christ does through us when we wait and hope expectantly, when we listen to His call and guidance as we meditate on His Word. God provides places to shine His light as we open our lives to serve others. He leads and empowers us to be His witnesses to the Gospel. We are reminded, "Therefore, we are ambassadors for Christ, God making His appeal through us. We implore you on behalf of Christ, be reconciled to God" (2 Corinthians 5:20).

We can act on His noble purposes because they are—and we are—from Him:

> For "In Him we live and move and have our being"; as even some of your own poets have said, "For we are indeed His offspring." (Acts 17:28)

I need, and continue to need, a push to live this out, to step past what is known and familiar, to take a little risk. I wrote this book to help, well, me. With my introverted self, I would be completely comfortable with just my books, hubby Raymond, my ninety-one-year-old mom who lives with us, and our loving church family. Not stepping out of my comfort zone but enjoying a small and tidy existence.

But my community needs me, and your community needs you. Our kind actions make a difference to others and to ourselves. Proverbs 11:25 provides an anchor for my heart and inspiration for this book: "Whoever brings blessing will be enriched, and one who waters will himself be watered." When we share Christ with others through our ordinary actions, the Holy Spirit opens their hearts to Jesus' light. Through us, He shines the grace of His Gospel and the truth of His Word for living.

As Christ shines through us, we bring hope to others. We bring joy to God and ourselves, which lifts our lives.

In this book, the word *shine* refers to our caring words and actions as a demonstration of our faith, as believers who are inspired, powered, and directed by the Holy Spirit. It is God working through us for good and for His glory. This is done mostly through small steps and ordinary actions, made extraordinary by the source, Jesus Christ. As noted theologian R. C. H. Lenski shares, "If our faith is the light, our works of faith are the rays that radiate from that light."[2] Exactly.

The word *lift* is defined here as "joy," "the raising of our spirits," "a bit of hope." (I'm ready for lift, aren't you?) *Lift* is the joy we feel when we serve Christ, when we realize how we fit into His plans, and when we see and sense His work being accomplished.

Hope reminds us of the special place Jesus has prepared for us in heaven.

The word *grace* celebrates preeminently God's unmerited favor, our unearned blessings, of forgiveness, life and salvation, given freely to us: "For by grace you have been saved through faith. And this is not your own doing; it is the gift of God, not a result of works so that no one may boast" (Ephesians

---

2   R. C. H. Lenski, *The Interpretation of St. Matthew's Gospel* (Minneapolis: Augsburg Publishing House, 1961), 203.

2:8–9). Secondly, as reflected in the title, we also celebrate God's *extraordinary grace* in the many spiritual gifts given to us, reflections of goodness and love; His gracious gifts of enablement to serve in various ways throughout our daily lives.

I'm thrilled you're here, reading and serving the Lord with me. This book is meant to be an instrument of spiritual discovery for both of us, to help expand our lives as believers and find new purpose in our every day. It can be used in a group setting, such as a Bible study, small group, or book club, or it can be enjoyed alone.

A road map for our journey together: Each chapter can serve as a weekly guide. Chapters are divided into specific focus areas, with biblical anchors and key themes for your focus. As you are able, connect and involve each person in the spiritual content. It was written to be welcoming and accessible to all.

The first two chapters of *Ordinary Lives, Extraordinary Grace* remind us of the glorious work God has done, His magnificent creation, His love for each of us, and our individually and spiritually directed purposes. Chapter 3 focuses on our spiritual foundations, and chapter 4 on how we can shine despite living in a fallen world. Chapter 5 celebrates worship. Chapter 6 explores healthy shining practices, with chapters 7, 8, and 9 focusing on our everyday shining spaces: our families and households, our neighbors and neighborhood, and our daily journeys out into our community. Chapter 10 is the big finish!

Each chapter begins with Scripture and is followed by a key spiritual takeaway. Each chapter closes with subject-related questions to ponder and discuss. An action challenge item provides a small-step, next-step way to shine. A special prayer completes and powers the segment.

The "Points to Ponder" section can be a rich time for discussion, fellowship, and personal contemplation. The questions are often deliberately open-ended to assist each reader in the journey of self-discovery for God's purposes. May the Holy Spirit guide you.

An essential housekeeping note: Shining the light of Christ describes the Spirit-led outpouring of healthy kindnesses, words, and deeds. This shining of Jesus' light, which is essential in our homes, neighborhoods, and communities today, is done with safe people in safe places in safe circumstances. If you're feeling the least bit unsure about your safety in any way, or if you do not know for certain that a person or situation is safe, the answer is no. God will lead you to an opportunity at another time and place.

As we begin, let's zoom in. Let's start in our homes and day-to-day journeys. Let's share kindness as we serve others and actively walk out our faith. Yes, we will discover new purpose. Yes, we will be lifted. Lift is a delightful benefit to the loving mindset and foundation of Christ-led caring and the extraordinary grace of God.

Our life situation, pathway, and vocations—amped and guided by the Holy Spirit—can be something powerful, whoever and wherever we are! When joined by our sisters and brothers in Christ, what joy and hope we can share as we serve those around us. Our ordinary ways seem unimportant to us, but the Holy Spirit makes them important. What blessings can be shared in our journeys and poured into our communities. What collective impact the Spirit will make through us together, all pointing back to our great God!

As we walk and stumble, step forward and back, let's embrace our next steps and take joy in the journey. My prayer is that you will be blessed by the reading of this book. Let's keep in touch via my website or social media. I'd love to hear about your study and adventures shining the light of Jesus!

May we serve together in the slow and small things. May we discover new purpose in our everyday lives and experience lift. May our actions benefit our homes and families, churches and neighborhoods, and give glory to God!

Soli Deo Gloria

CHAPTER 1
YOU ARE UNIQUE AND PRECIOUS

BIBLICAL ANCHOR: PSALM 139:13–16

For You formed my inward parts; You knitted me together in my mother's womb. I praise You, for I am fearfully and wonderfully made. Wonderful are Your works; my soul knows it very well. My frame was not hidden from You, when I was being made in secret, intricately woven in the depths of the earth. Your eyes saw my unformed substance; in Your book were written, every one of them, the days that were formed for me, when as yet there was none of them.

KEY TAKEAWAY

God created a spectacular universe and each spectacular human being. You are an original creation, a one-of-a-kind you, unique and precious, and deeply loved. The Holy Spirit lives in each believer as a God-given helper, guide, coach, and strength-provider for our individual journeys. Each believer has a divine purpose to help build the Kingdom.

One-of-a-Kind World

Our world is a big place, with more than eight billion people living on earth.[3] Sometimes it's easy to feel small and

---

3 "Day of Eight Billion, 15 November 2022," United Nations, November 1, 2022, https://www.un.org/development/desa/pd/events/day-eight-billion (accessed December 10, 2022).

insignificant when we consider the number of living human beings. It's another prophecy fulfilled, as God told Adam and Eve and later shared with Noah: "And God blessed them. And God said to them, 'Be fruitful and multiply and fill the earth and subdue it'" (Genesis 1:28; see 9:1).

We have an incredible home. It's kept in cyclical rhythms and balance by a small, lifeless moon that's ours alone.[4] Our life on earth is sustained and held in place by a star that is 96 million miles away, in perfect orbit—not too close and not too far away—and with just the right amount of light. Can you imagine God at creation, putting the sun in place? "Okay, a little farther . . . yep, that's just the right distance away from the earth—perfect. And let's set the temp at 27 million degrees, just right to sustain My people and their planet."[5] Amazing.

Breathtaking evidence of our vast universe can be seen through scientific advances, including images from NASA's Hubble and Webb space telescopes, the Mars remote-controlled rovers, and other space missions. We continue to discover the enormity of God's handiwork and witness more pieces of it.

Our planet contains greatly varied geographies and diversity of plants, animals, and other living things. Just think about it. All the different plants, from the lily to the cactus to the tomato. All the different animals, from the hippo to the eagle to the mouse. A multitude of trees. All the smaller creations, the butterfly, bumblebee, and ant. And the smallest, including microscopic organisms, molecules, quarks, electrons, and protons. Such diversity!

---

4   "Moon Facts," NASA, https://science.nasa.gov/moon/facts/ (accessed January 15, 2024).
5   "Our Sun: Facts," NASA, https://science.nasa.gov/sun/facts/#hds-sidebar -nav-3 (accessed January 15, 2024).

Have you ever visited the beach or the mountains or some other natural space and felt in awe of God's creative power? Even in your backyard, consider the variety and beauty of the local birds, plants, and trees that you may be blessed to have around you. Consider the daily art show of a sunrise or sunset. Even everyday occurrences are pretty miraculous.

Scientists estimate about 9 million unique "eukaryote" species exist on earth, meaning "organisms that have cells containing complex structures within membranes."[6] Wow, God!

One-of-a-Kind Human Being

The complexity of God's creation continues delightfully forward to include every human being. You likely know that no two humans have the same fingerprints. Additionally, our fingerprints vary between our fingers, meaning we have a unique print on each finger.[7] We can rejoice in our unique creation.

According to the Population Reference Bureau, our current living population is 7 percent of the estimated 117 billion humans ever born.[8] That's quite a few fingerprints.

There's more. Beyond our DNA and fingerprints, each person's facial structure, eye characteristics, and vocal patterns are individualized identifiers. Scientists also believe we each give off a combination of smells, creating a "thermal plume"

---

6   J. J. Wiens, "How Many Species Are There on Earth? Progress and Problems," *PLOS Biology*, November 20, 2023, https://doi.org/10.1371/journal.pbio.3002388 (accessed December 8, 2023).

7   "A Simplified Guide to Fingerprint Analysis," Global Forensic and Justice Center, https://www.forensicsciencesimplified.org/prints (accessed December 8, 2023).

8   "How Many People Have Ever Lived on Earth?," Population Reference Bureau, November 15, 2022, https://www.prb.org/articles/how-many-people-have-ever-lived-on-earth/ (accessed November 19, 2022).

that's ours alone. Other areas of biometric identification being studied include the shape of our ears and backsides, our cardiac patterns, the way we walk, and the shape and vibration of our skulls.[9] Remarkable.

As the creation story unfolds in the book of Genesis, we see that God created a lush planet filled with plants, animals, and other living things in a just-right natural setting. As His last, most satisfying work, God fashioned Adam and Eve and started the human race. We can wonder at and rejoice that God chose to create us in His own image (Genesis 1:27).

As image-bearers of God, we have incredible bodies. Consider these discoveries:

- Messages from our brain can travel at speeds of up to 200 miles per hour.

- Our brain has 86 million nerve cells and 100 trillion connections.

- Our hearts will beat more than 3 billion times during our lives.

- Our blood circulates about 12,000 miles a day.

- We breathe more than 20,000 times a day.[10]

These facts are just a small selection from the blockbuster story of the human body. Our birth and growth, emotions and memory, capabilities and functionality, higher level thoughts

9   Richard Gray, "The Seven Ways You Are Totally Unique," British Broadcasting Corporation, January 10, 2017, https://www.bbc.com /future/article/20170109-the-seven-ways-you-are-totally-unique (accessed November 19, 2022).

10 Karin Lehnardt, "92 Amazing Human Body Facts," FactRetriever (website), updated January 22, 2022, https://www.factretriever.com /body-facts (accessed November 20, 2022).

and actions are all wrapped into God-created, individualized people packages.

Most important, God gave us souls for an earthly and eternal existence in heaven with Him by faith in His Son. Although He longs for each one of us to spend eternity with Him, some of us, unfortunately, choose otherwise. None of this happened by accident. It's all part of God's extraordinary plan: from creation to the redemptive death on the cross and resurrection of His innocent Son, Jesus, to save us from our sins, death, and the devil.

God has good plans for our individual lives too, as we see in the book of Jeremiah: "Before I formed you in the womb I knew you, and before you were born I consecrated you; I appointed you a prophet to the nations" (1:5). Not everyone will be a prophet like Jeremiah, but all believers are called to serve God in special ways.

There has never been a repeat person. Every human life is created by God as a unique individual. You're the only you, ever!

One-of-a-Kind Helper

And there's more to this exciting story; we've saved the best for last. Perhaps the most miraculous feature in all creation is that God lives within believers through the indwelling of the Holy Spirit. How cool is that?

Through the gift of faith, which God creates in us through the Gospel of Jesus, the Holy Spirit makes a home in our hearts, and we become a holy temple (house of worship). As 1 Corinthians 3:16 explains: "Do you not know that you are God's temple and that God's Spirit dwells in you?" What a privilege!

How did this come about? Once again, there was an amazing and specific plan. Before His death, Jesus shared the news that the Spirit would come as a Helper in our daily walk:

These things I have spoken to you while I am still with you. But the Helper, the Holy Spirit, whom the Father will send in My name, He will teach you all things and bring to your remembrance all that I have said to you. (John 14:25–26)

The Holy Spirit is a light to our spirit and the coach of our hearts, living within each believer as helper, advocate, and counselor. We can rely on this power to open the meaning of Scripture, discern God's will as made known through His commandments, lead in truth, intercede, convict us of our sin, comfort and renew, and make us holy. The Spirit knows how to make us shine, leading and nudging (okay, sometimes pushing) us forward for the good purposes of God.

This power yields spiritual fruit when we open ourselves to its guidance, leading us to live as lights in the every day:

The fruit of the Spirit is love, joy, peace, patience, kindness, goodness, faithfulness, gentleness, self-control; against such things there is no law. (Galatians 5:22–23)

Sometimes I blow it when the Spirit nudges me to do something good. I miss the opportunity or get uncomfortable and run from purpose. Sometimes my selfish nature rules the day. When this happens, I can confess my mistakes to God. Share my sorrow. Ask for His forgiveness and new strength, knowing that He provides this Holy Spirit–powered operating system to help me navigate daily life as I live in God's will in accordance with His commandments, despite my failings. Even in our imperfections, God is in us and with us, everywhere we go!

Martin Luther, in his life- and world-changing writings, commended prayer, meditation on the Word, and spiritual testing as ways for people to mature as Christ-followers.[11] When we read, consider, and meditate on the Bible, the Spirit fills us with power, wisdom, knowledge, and understanding of the Word. We grow spiritually. When we pray to our heavenly Father in Jesus' name, we are further connected, empowered, and guided by the Holy Spirit.

Through the Word and sacraments of Baptism and the Lord's Supper—the means of grace—we receive God's wonderful gifts of forgiveness, faith, and eternal life. We are spiritually fed, strengthened, and equipped. We grow in mercy, knowledge, maturity, understanding, purpose, and alignment with His will. Author and speaker Christina Hergenrader encourages us:

> May you live the life you have been given. May you turn to prayer constantly. May you keep burrowing deeper into His Word to find real strength. May your very life and all you create give glory to the one true Savior. May you notice the ways the Spirit nudges you toward the gifts of real goodness, divine patience, and deep love.[12]

---

11 See Martin Luther, "Preface to the Wittenberg Edition of Luther's German Writings," in *Luther's Works*, American Edition, vol. 34, *Career of the Reformer IV*, ed. Jaroslav Jan Pelikan, Hilton C. Oswald, and Helmut T. Lehmann (Philadelphia: Fortress Press, 1960), 285–87.

12 Christina Hergenrader, *Inspired by the Holy Spirit: Four Habits for Faithful Living* (St. Louis: Concordia Publishing House, 2021), 18.

One-of-a-Kind History

What about within our lives? A pattern of individual purpose is demonstrated throughout the Bible in the lives, families, and circumstances of God's people. We witness details of faithful men and women who served a specific charge from the Lord, uniquely when and where He placed their lives in history. Consider these key figures:

- *Hagar*: As a powerless slave, Hagar suffered from the misguided actions and resentment of others and was cast out of Abraham's household into the wilderness. Overcome by despair, she cried out. God heard her cry and sent an angel to reassure, encourage, and direct her as she mothered Ishmael, who went on to be the leader of a new nation. Her lovely naming of God as the "God of seeing" (Genesis 16:13) is a testimony to all of us.

- *Joseph*: From a favorite son of Jacob to a slave to a prisoner, Joseph experienced a dramatic and negative change in his circumstances. God was present throughout his adversity to fortify Joseph's faith so he could persevere to His purpose. Joseph's God-given gift of dream interpretation provided the way out of jail and elevation to the top leader under Pharaoh. By placing Joseph in this position, God saved Joseph's family (a remnant of God's chosen people), established him in his adopted home of Egypt, and preserved many souls in the surrounding countries from famine (Genesis 41). Through Joseph's dealings with his brothers, God also demonstrated the power of repentance, grace, and forgiveness.

- *Moses:* The unlikely infant survivor of a murderous edict, Moses was rescued from the Nile River and raised as an Egyptian prince. He suffered a personal reversal of fortune through his own murderous act. Although Moses became an off-the-grid shepherd, God worked through him to lead the Israelites out of slavery and out of Egypt. Indeed, Moses was perfectly experienced and uniquely placed to assist as God freed His people from Pharaoh (see Exodus 2–3).

- *Rahab:* Rahab was not only a prostitute but also a Canaanite and an enemy of Israel. But when she heard how God had delivered Israel from Egypt, the Spirit raised her up to testify in faith to the Lord's power and to help God's people. As the Israelites prepared to invade Jericho, Rahab assisted their cause with courage. The Lord even led her to be part of the lineage of Jesus as the mother of Boaz (see Joshua 2:1–21; Matthew 1:5–6).

- *David:* David was filled with the Holy Spirit when he was anointed by the prophet Samuel (1 Samuel 16:13). Though David was an insignificant shepherd serving out in the fields and the youngest of seven more physically impressive brothers, God chose this "man after My heart" (Acts 13:22). The Spirit empowered David to slay the giant Goliath and later become king of Israel.

- *Esther:* This beautiful Jewish orphan girl was continually guided by the counsel and direction of her faithful cousin Mordecai and others. During the rule of King Ahasuerus, and through a special set of circumstances, the Lord led Esther to become queen and emerge as a heroic leader. Esther's brave actions—bold with purpose and devotion—saved God's chosen people from annihilation in early Persia.

The Bible is filled with inspirational stories of imperfect, ordinary people who were chosen by God to be His extraordinary instruments as He accomplished His will here on earth.

Now you might be thinking, as I have, "Well, those people, they're in the Bible. They were special. That's different and long ago. I'm just an imperfect, ordinary person in a crowded, noisy world."

But God delights in doing unexpected great things through people. He empowers and leads ordinary folk—like you and me—through the Spirit to serve. No one is beyond reach for God's purposes!

I used to think I had to be important or famous or have a certain notoriety or particular career to impact the lives of others. But I was wrong.

We are all part of God's spectacular creation in this day, at this time. You're a unique human being with a specific place in the world. And, like many biblical figures, you have your own history, which may include a difficult upbringing, reversal of circumstances, unwelcome storylines, failures, and present-day challenges. God has the power to weave the dark aspects of our backgrounds into His light-filled purposes.

Despite anything and everything, God has good plans for you and for me. This modern paraphrase of Isaiah 54:10 seems to be everywhere on the internet, and it sums it up well: "How cool is it that the same God who created the oceans and the mountains and the stars thought the world needed **you** too."

POINTS TO PONDER (INDIVIDUALLY OR IN A SMALL GROUP, BOOK CLUB, OR BIBLE STUDY)

- How have you been reminded of the enormity, diversity, and individuality of God's creation?

- What are some examples of how God has made you (yes, lovely you) His one-of-a-kind creation?

- List some examples of how God is using you for His purposes here on earth today.

ACTION CHALLENGE

- Thank God for His creation, including your favorite aspects of it.

- Contemplate how you are uniquely created and placed.

- Meditate on the enormity of our world and also on God's specific love and attention for you as an individual.

PRAYER

Dear heavenly Father, we are in awe of Your creation of the universe and Your creation of each one of us. We celebrate Your magnificent artistry and vast, complex work. What a wonderful world You made for us! Forgive us for failing to treasure the uniqueness and the beauty of our earthly home. Thank You for creating us to be one-of-a-kind people. Thank You for sending Your beloved Son to redeem us and cherish us individually. Help us to treasure Your creation, including ourselves, as we serve Your purposes. In Jesus' name. Amen.

CHAPTER 2
YOU WERE CREATED FOR GOOD PURPOSES

BIBLICAL ANCHOR: EPHESIANS 2:8-10

For by grace you have been saved through faith. And this is not your own doing; it is the gift of God, not a result of works, so that no one may boast. For we are His workmanship, created in Christ Jesus for good works, which God prepared beforehand, that we should walk in them.

KEY TAKEAWAY

God saves you by grace through faith in Jesus, who completed the work of salvation for you and all humanity on the cross. He gives you work to serve others in His name. God has specific plans for your life in the way He created you and where He placed you. He blesses each of our lives with Kingdom purposes, empowering us through the presence of the Holy Spirit to serve Him and others.

About Vocation

Vocation, for our purposes today, is an understanding that God has many different callings and purposes for our lives. He reveals these to us by His Spirit. We often see these gifts identified and encouraged in our lives by those close to us, that is, other believers who notice how God has prepared us to serve.

Vocations are unique for each person and can include serving as a spouse, parent, neighbor, child, worker, citizen, and other important roles in our daily lives. We are called individually to these multiple and divinely determined life roles. Vocations can change and grow as we live, age, and learn. In his landmark book *God at Work: Your Christian Vocation in All of Life*, author Gene Veith summarizes vocation beautifully:

> God—making use of your family and your culture—created you as you are. The doctrine of vocation has to do with the mystery of individuality, how God creates each human being to be different from all of the rest and gives each a unique calling in every stage of life. Thus you have particular talents, which you are to understand are His gifts. You have a particular personality, with interests, likes, and dislikes that not everyone shares. Such is the plenitude of God's creation that no two people— or snowflakes or leaves or anything God has made—are exactly alike. Vocations are likewise unique, with no two people taking up exactly the same space in the family, the nation, the church, or the workplace. Finding your vocation, then, has to do, in part, with finding your God-given talents (what you can do) and your God-given personality (what fits the person you are).[13]

It is also important to note that all vocations are equal in status before God.[14] We don't have to worry about whether what we do or how we serve is more or less valuable than that of another person. Different people, different functions, same

---

13 Gene Edward Veith Jr., *God at Work: Your Christian Vocation in All of Life* (Wheaton, IL: Crossway, Copyright © 2002), 52–53. Used by permission of Crossway, a publishing ministry of Good News Publishers, Wheaton, IL 60187, www.crossway.org.
14 See Veith, *God at Work*, 50.

importance. Similarly, as in our bodies, a foot or hand or eye or ear is not better than any other body part; all are valuable and purposeful as integral functioning parts of the whole. We work together, as "the body does not consist of one member but of many" (1 Corinthians 12:14; see also vv. 15–27).

Every believer has an important function in God's plan as part of the Body of Christ. We see this theme again in Ephesians 4:15–16: "Christ, from whom the whole body, joined and held together by every joint with which it is equipped, when each part is working properly, makes the body grow so that it builds itself up in love."

I see God's great plan lived out in my husband, my mom, and our three adult children. They are unique individuals blessed with unique talents and experiences, uniquely serving their families and communities. Uniquely loved!

Veith also reminds us of the origin of our vocations: "Despite what our culture leads us to believe, *vocation is not self-chosen*. That is to say, we do not *choose* our vocations. We are *called* to them. There is a big difference."[15] This, too, I see in my family—how each member was created beautifully and individually. How each beloved one serves today through innate gifts, education, and life experiences.

For me, if I wasn't going to become a cowgirl (which was my childhood dream), I was going to be a writer. Each twist and turn of my life journey *has* included writing. It's what I do and what I've always done, called by the Lord.

Author Margo Heath-Dupre adds further insight:

> God speaks to all of humanity in His Word, the Bible; however, through our personal study of Scripture, God

---

15 Veith, *God at Work*, 50. Emphasis in original.

is speaking directly to us. He is communing with us individually because His will for our life is personal; He placed us in this time and place and created us with vocations that we use to serve Him and benefit others.[16]

We each have our own path to walk and our own way to serve as a follower of Jesus. You, with your own talents, place, and vocations, are an important part of creation and a unique member of the Body of Christ! Go you!

Walking the Walk

Sometimes we may wonder what exactly God wants us to do next. How does He want us to serve? How will we know His plans for us?

Each of us has purpose. God works through the Holy Spirit to lead us to specific and sometimes surprising places and vocations.

My husband, Raymond, is a second-career pastor. At the age of forty-nine, he answered God's call to enter the seminary to become a pastor. He left a prestigious position as part of the federal government's Senior Executive Service in Washington, DC, to pursue this calling. I am honored to stand by his side. The road hasn't been easy, but it has provided service, growth, and joy. God's redirection in our lives was unexpected but welcome. Past vocations supported the new places God led us to serve.

God calls believers to specific ministries and utilizes our lives to spread the saving Gospel of Jesus across the country

---

16 Margo Heath-Dupre, *Be Thou My Guide: A Bible Study on Trusting God* (St. Louis: Concordia Publishing House, 2020), 32.

and the globe. He also often guides us to local "curbside service" places where we can share His love and message right where we are. It's a both-and mission, right here and over there. God can use our lives in far-off places and in ordinary, nearby spaces for His purposes, as we live, interact with, and walk our life path.

As we seek to please God and follow His commandments in our every day, goodwill flows from our actions. We speak kindly to those around us. We pay attention; we listen. We help those we encounter with our eyes open. We not only live in His love, guided by His love, but we also share His love with those around us through our visible actions.

Empowered by His divine grace, we are given good purposes: "For God will insist on this in sum: if you obey Him, offering love and service, He will reward you abundantly with all good."[17] Yes, even you, even me!

Consider these surprising individuals described in biblical accounts, as Jesus ministers to people in the everyday steps of His earthly journey. Not kings. Not influencers. Just ordinary people who experienced the Divine in person:

- *Ten men with leprosy (Luke 17:11–19)*: As Jesus entered a village, He met ten men who had leprosy (and thus were outcasts). The men stood at a distance and called, "Jesus, Master, have mercy on us." Jesus cleansed and healed the ten, but only the Samaritan (the outsider and foreigner) turned back to fall at Jesus' feet, worshiping and thanking Him for healing.

- *A widow's son (Luke 7:11–17)*: As Jesus was traveling, He noticed a funeral procession for a widow's only

---

17 Luther's Large Catechism, Part 1, paragraph 136.

son. Filled with compassion, Jesus stepped into the situation and brought the woman's son back to life: "Young man, I say to you, arise." Jesus just "happened" to be in the neighborhood. He met a parade of death and made it a parade of life.

- A *woman at a well* (*John 4:1–26*): At a Samaritan village well, Jesus encountered a woman. (Samaritans were perceived as enemies of the Jewish people.) This Samaritan woman had had five husbands and currently lived with a man who was not her husband. Surprisingly, Jesus revealed Himself to her as the Messiah: "I who speak to you am He." This encounter became a mission explosion, as the testimony from this woman—though a community outcast—opened many hearts to Jesus' message.

We, too, as servants of the Lord, look for opportunities to serve in Jesus' name on our earthly journeys.

Years ago, I remember Connie Denninger, my pastor's wife, sharing this wisdom: whenever she went somewhere, met someone, or experienced a situation, she would keep an open, prayerful, and curious heart with an attitude of "I wonder what God is doing, how He is going to lead and use me." Beautiful.

We can be hopeful and available as we watch and listen for the Lord's guidance, trusting that He will provide ways for us to uniquely serve. He can use our errands and classes and appointments and encounters for His heavenly purposes in our everyday, ordinary lives. Yes, He can—and He does!

Location, Location, Location

Let's look at more instances when our Lord lived out this concept of serving where God places or leads.

In Acts 8:26–40, we see an angel of the Lord prompt Philip to "rise and go toward the south to the road that goes down from Jerusalem to Gaza." Philip listened and did as the angel asked. On that road, he encountered an Ethiopian man who was a eunuch and court official of Candace, queen of the Ethiopians. The man was puzzling out a verse from the prophet Isaiah.

Philip explained the passage and shared the Good News about Jesus. The Ethiopian replied, "See, here is water! What prevents me from being baptized?" He's like, "Hey, I believe; let's take care of this right here, right now." Through Philip, the Lord provided answers to a yearning heart and inspired a Baptism, creating a mission-driven believer from another land. God was aware of the Ethiopian man's location and spiritual yearning. Through an angel, He sent Philip to meet that need. And through the newly baptized man, He sent the Gospel to Ethiopia.

In the Gospel of Luke, Jesus tells the well-known parable of the Good Samaritan in answer to the question "Who is my neighbor?"

> A man was going down from Jerusalem to Jericho, and he fell among robbers, who stripped him and beat him and departed, leaving him half dead. Now by chance, a priest was going down that road, and when he saw him he passed by on the other side. So likewise a Levite, when he came to the place and saw him, passed by on the other side. But a Samaritan, as he journeyed, came

to where he was, and when he saw him, he had compassion. He went to him and bound up his wounds, pouring on oil and wine. Then he set him on his own animal and brought him to an inn and took care of him. And the next day he took out two denarii and gave them to the innkeeper, saying, "Take care of him, and whatever more you spend, I will repay you when I come back." Which of these three, do you think, proved to be a neighbor to the man who fell among the robbers? The man who had asked the question replied, "The one who showed him mercy," to which Jesus replied, "You go, and do likewise." (Luke 10:30–37)

Jesus' teaching paints a picture in which a Samaritan graciously and generously served someone—an enemy—who was literally in his path. The "important" folks, religious leaders, just passed by. The cultural outsider inconvenienced himself and was willing to help another in need during his journey.

We can also look to the apostle Paul, who led an adventurous ministry life to the Gentiles and served in unusual places during three missionary journeys. Even when confined in prison, his time was fruitful for spreading the Gospel of the Lord to the other inmates and jail guards. He had time to write to the early churches, to teach and encourage their growing faith and mission. Because Paul was captive, new leaders had to be raised up in his stead to travel, preach, and teach during this imprisonment (see Acts 28:30–31 and Philippians 1:12–18). Wherever he was, Paul shared his faith and impacted many lives for the Lord.

In addition to our unique creation and our specific vocations, our location is key—where we live, work, volunteer, and travel. As in His earthly ministry, Christ is working through us to help others in our day-to-day journeys too. His purposes are accomplished in the daily lives of those who serve Him, wherever we are, wherever we go.

Redefining What's Important

Part of our discussion together includes rethinking what's important. Over the years, I've needed to adjust my own ideas. When I was a young adult just out of college, my goal was to achieve worldly significance. I headed to the Washington, DC, political scene and worked long hours chasing power and advancement. I believed that my life would be valuable if I became important.

God provided remarkable experiences for me to serve Him in that place: great jobs supporting political engagement in my vocations of citizen and voter. He allowed me to serve a newly elected US president as part of his presidential transition team. I also served as a writer in support of the president and other political leaders as a part of the inside-the-beltway crowd. Sadly, I placed too much importance on that setting, valuing my work and contribution above the efforts of others, thinking high status meant higher worth. (It's painful to write this, but true.)

Thankfully, my thinking has expanded beyond those limitations. Through living and learning then and in the following decades, I learned how God treasures and utilizes circumstances, both large and small, good and bad, according to His purposes in all our lives. What God sees as important does not always match what the world sees as important.

My time and experiences in DC were valuable, both then and in my ordinary life today. The spaces and places where God has led you are likewise valuable to where you are now. Romans 8:28 reminds us: "We know that for those who love God all things work together for good, for those who are called according to His purpose."

God's Word and our lives reveal unlikely all-stars. God delights in the smallest of details and situations for His kingdom work. In majesty and great love, He values little children, the elderly, the forgotten, the invisible, and even little, insignificant me. As the sweet hymn shares, "God loves me dearly, loves even me" (*LSB* 392).

Today I know that, even as an ordinary person and daily sinner, my self-worth is anchored in the fact that God created me, made me His beloved, and redeemed me through Christ. There is nothing for me to do or achieve to receive this unconditional love and saving grace. Just as I am, I am valued as His precious child. No high status required!

There are many instances in the Bible where Jesus illustrated this point and turned the culture upside down, deliberately choosing unlikely, unimportant people instead of the folks most valued by the culture:

> **For consider your calling, brothers: not many of you were wise according to worldly standards, not many were powerful, not many were of noble birth. But God chose what is foolish in the world to shame the wise; God chose what is weak in the world to shame the strong; God chose what is low and despised in the world, even things that are not, to bring to nothing things that are, so that no human being might boast**

in the presence of God. And because of Him you are in Christ Jesus, who became to us wisdom from God, righteousness and sanctification and redemption, so that, as it is written, "Let the one who boasts, boast in the Lord." (1 Corinthians 1:26–31)

In Jesus' earthly ministry, He often reached out to known sinners, outsiders, insignificant people, and unpopular people as part of His purpose. In contrast to the culture of that day and even our culture today, He most often gazed down the social hierarchy. Consider these Bible stories, preserved for us to read, study, and inspire:

- A *cheating, hated tax collector* (*Luke 19:1–10*): Jesus encountered Zacchaeus in Jericho and invited Himself over to dinner. The locals couldn't believe that the Lord would be a guest of such a man. Zacchaeus surprised everyone with his exclamation, "Behold, Lord, the half of my goods I give to the poor. And if I have defrauded anyone of anything, I restore it fourfold." As Jesus explained, "The Son of Man came to seek and to save the lost." We are all lost people needing a Savior.

- A *sinful woman* (*Luke 7:36–50*): Jesus was eating at a Pharisee's house when a woman who was known to be a sinner entered, wept at Jesus' feet, and then kissed and anointed His feet with ointment. Jesus astounded the room by accepting her presence and forgiving her sins: "Your faith has saved you; go in peace." His act shocked nearby religious leaders. We, too, can be accepted in faith by the Lord, no matter what we've done, as repentance and His forgiveness free us from our past.

- A *thief on a cross* (*Luke 23:39–43*): This unnamed man was a criminal. And yet, he came to faith on the cross: "Jesus, remember me when You come into Your kingdom." Jesus replied, "Truly, I say to you, today you will be with Me in paradise." This story is included in the Bible for us to read and remember that no one is beyond forgiveness or salvation. No one who calls upon Jesus for rescue will be without His care.

Even Jesus' arrival into our world was a surprising and humble entrance for the Savior of the world, as He was born as a human baby in a stable, among the hay and animals. Jesus' disciples were mostly everyday people, not high-status leaders. Fishermen and shepherds were not high on the social scale.

Our culture today highly values those who are famous, important, rich, and powerful. We might even be convinced that our lives aren't very important when compared to the lives of brilliant spiritual leaders and public figures. Yes, let's be inspired by good teachings and examples. But let's not live as spectators. God has good work for you and me to do.

Again and again, God works out His incredible purposes through all kinds of people. Unpopular people. Sinners. Outsiders. Everyday people like you and me. Even in the small stories, we see transformation take place. What is important to the world is often different than what is important to God. Then and now!

When God moves His people into place, small purpose is still great purpose. "Unimportant" can be very important indeed. Take time to see the good purpose in your life. God can use your life and vocations to serve Him in our hurting world. Ordinary can be extraordinary!

POINTS TO PONDER (INDIVIDUALLY OR IN A SMALL GROUP, BOOK CLUB, OR BIBLE STUDY)

- What are your various vocations? How do you serve others today in these vocations? (Vocations can include but are not limited to being a parent, child, sibling, volunteer, employee, boss, church member, citizen, and neighbor.)

- How have you seen or experienced helpful actions of others that may have seemed ordinary but were, in fact, extraordinary?

- Do you see yourself as an important instrument of the Lord in your daily life? Why or why not? Are you open to His leading?

ACTION CHALLENGE

- Thank God once again for the ways He has uniquely created and placed you. Treasure your vocations.

- Consider and share an ordinary occurrence that became extraordinary for you.

- Note people nearby who can benefit from your everyday kindness. Do you believe they are important to God? Pray to be led in a first or additional step.

PRAYER

Dear gracious heavenly Father. We can't even comprehend how You created our complex world and each and every one of us. Wow! And thank You. We are honored to serve You in the places and spaces we live in today. Forgive us for not noticing Your small but important aims right where we are. Open our eyes to our unique vocations, how we might shine Your light in Your extraordinary way as we journey through our ordinary lives. In the name of Your precious Son, Jesus. Amen.

CHAPTER 3
SPIRITUALLY ANCHORED

BIBLICAL ANCHOR: COLOSSIANS 2:6–7

Therefore, as you received Christ Jesus the Lord, so walk in Him, rooted and built up in Him and established in the faith, just as you were taught, abounding in thanksgiving.

KEY TAKEAWAY

Anchoring ourselves spiritually is job number one as we shine the light of Jesus. As we worship, pray, and study the Word, the Holy Spirit strengthens, empowers, and leads us to important work, whoever we are and wherever we are. By staying connected to the Lord and offering up our lives, we thrive and produce spiritual fruit.

What It Means to Be Anchored

I love church paraments. Paraments are the beautiful fabric hangings that adorn the altar, lectern, and pulpit, and the vestments worn by the pastor or priest. They can be embroidered, appliqued, or painted with sacred, spiritual symbols—holy art—representing the seasons in the Church Year and reminding us of our core beliefs. Some churches don't use paraments and are more informal. At our church, one of our paraments is embroidered with an anchor. Why?

The anchor signifies that our faith is firmly secured to Christ. We are held fast. We surrender to God's purposes for our lives and His callings, not our own will or our own plans for the future. Anchoring means that, in faith, through the work of the Holy Spirit, we embrace the sweet Gospel message and the call of Jesus, our Lord.

Our anchoring is strengthened as we daily live in God's love. The Holy Spirit keeps this connection vibrant through our reading of the living Word of God, taking time to worship in church, partaking in the Lord's Supper regularly, and spending time in prayer. Spiritual engagement leads to a sanctified life: a continuing spiritual connection informs, guides, and powers our day-to-day service. As we are anchored, we are guided to new and important work that the Lord determines.

Author and nationally recognized consultant Kurt Senske shares his own process: "As I prayerfully discern how I am to be of service to my neighbor, God speaks to me through my Baptism, daily reading of His Word, worship, and the Lord's Table, enabling me to discern the calling that is uniquely mine."[18]

As we stay plugged in and connected, God provides us with the power and the specific purpose for our lives: "But the Helper, the Holy Spirit, whom the Father will send in My name, He will teach you all things and bring to your remembrance all that I have said to you" (John 14:26).

In my own life, sometimes I drift off and pursue my own "excellent" plans, rushing ahead with activities and goals without reaching out to God for guidance. Or I make plans and then ask God to bless them. (Eek!) Sometimes I forget that God's plan is better than mine could ever be. When I get it right, it is because I have surrendered to the workings of the Holy Spirit.

---

18 Kurt Senske, *The CEO and the Board: The Art of Nonprofit Governance as a Competitive Advantage* (St. Louis: Concordia Publishing House, 2023), 137.

Although it feels oppositional to our intellect and strategies, offering up our lives to God creates a miraculously superior result. Why? Because we can trust and rely on God to care about what we do, to lead us to and through our vocations, and to provide the power we need to accomplish His will through the Holy Spirit. Yes!

By being anchored—especially by reading God's Word—we connect to God's help. We are freed from our own foolishness for His beautiful purposes. We are able to shine!

Connected by Grace

God generously created additional means for humanity to connect with and receive His love, direction, power, and strength. Let's consider the key ways God's means of grace are available to anchor us:

- *Through confession and the forgiveness of sins:* When we confess our sins, God hears us and provides forgiveness, cleansing our hearts and putting us right with Him. We sin daily, so the process is ongoing. My pastor husband likes to call it "the spiritual washing machine." (Like our home washing machine, both are going all the time!)

- *Through Baptism:* The power is God working to wash away sin—the Word plus water at His command. God claims us and saves us as His precious children, and we become part of His family and the Body of Christ. We find a precious place of belonging. We are freed from the power of sin, death, and the devil.

- *Through the Lord's Supper:* God strengthens us through the body and blood of Christ in, with, and under the bread and wine in Communion. In remembrance of Him and through this sacred and mysterious practice, we are strengthened by the Holy Spirit for our daily walk and assured of forgiveness, life, and salvation.

- *By gathering together with other believers:* We receive spiritual power when we are involved in "the mutual conversation and consolation of brethren" (Smalcald Articles, Part III, Article IV). We are encouraged and strengthened in the Holy Spirit when together we worship, gather in fellowship, pray, and practice repentance, confession, and forgiveness.

God in His great mercy has provided key ways for us to stay connected, to live as forgiven people, to be empowered by Him, and to be built up with and by other believers as we live in community. His amazing grace connects it all!

Prayers Up

Prayer is an essential and powerful part of our faith walk. It's a two-way conversation, talking to God in Jesus' name. We share what is on our hearts, and He always hears us. We can still ourselves in quietness and faith to listen for guidance from God. As temples of the Holy Spirit, we are portable prayer units—we can pray whenever and wherever we go!

And we are encouraged in the beautiful hymn "What a Friend We Have in Jesus":

Have we trials and temptations?

    Is there trouble anywhere?

We should never be discouraged—
    Take it to the Lord in prayer.
Can we find a friend so faithful
    Who will all our sorrows share?
Jesus knows our every weakness—
    Take it to the Lord in prayer. (*LSB* 770:2)

Prayer is always available. We can pray in many ways and in any circumstance. Perhaps you already have your own lovely way to pray. The ACTS method is widely utilized in Christian communities today; it is my go-to:

1. *Adoration of God*: We begin our praise with Bible verses, hymn stanzas, our own words, or a combo pack. We have evidence of His greatness all around us, including in the miracle of our creation and the wondrous world He created for us. A soul-full experience!

2. *Confession*: Yep. We confess who we are as sinners. Things we did or didn't do. Sometimes the Spirit leads me to confess something I hadn't thought of confessing but I need to own up to. It's freeing to give our sins to God and receive His complete forgiveness. I'm good at hanging on to my mistakes and sins, reliving the pain and shame over and over. But God says they are gone "as far as the east is from the west" (Psalm 103:12).

3. *Thanksgiving*: God has blessed us. Even with the challenges of life, we have much to be thankful for. It is just and right to thank God for everything we can think of in our lives and families—for answered prayer and for the many ways He provides for us, cares for us, leads us, and loves us. What are you grateful for today? Start with the small things. (Studies have shown that expressing

thanks brings mental and physical benefits. Why not thank the giver of all good things?)[19]

4. *Supplication*: This is the "help me" section. This used to be my main prayer; you know, a shopping list of everyone who needed help and all my concerns, struggles, challenges, and dreams. Prayer is balanced when our requests for help are part of an overall prayer time, not the main theme. Although God knows all our needs before we say a word, He desires us to communicate with Him in prayer, as His children. Share yourself with your Creator!

Prayer is a rich, powerful resource, and it connects us to God's good and perfect will. It is a time of sharing anything and everything with our dear loving heavenly Father. Save time for simply listening. Claim the promise that God speaks to us as we meditate on His Word:

Do not be conformed to this world, but be transformed by the renewal of your mind, that by testing you may discern what is the will of God, what is good and acceptable and perfect. (Romans 12:2)

Isn't it convenient that we can pray to God at any time? Prayer can be as simple as "Help me, God." Or, as we learned from a sweet little old lady in a nursing home, "I need You, Jesus. Amen." We can say the Lord's Prayer, as Jesus taught us. Or a morning or evening prayer. We can "pray without ceasing" (1 Thessalonians 5:17). There are so many ways to pray!

19 Robert A. Emmons and Michael E. McCullough, "Counting Blessings Versus Burdens: An Experimental Investigation of Gratitude and Subjective Well-Being in Daily Life," *Journal of Personality and Social Psychology* 84, no. 2 (2003): 377–89, https://greatergood.berkeley.edu /pdfs/GratitudePDFs/6Emmons-BlessingsBurdens.pdf.

Especially in our fear or terror or emergency, we can call on God for help. He promises to be with us through anything and everything: "Have I not commanded you? Be strong and courageous. Do not be frightened, and do not be dismayed, for the LORD your God is with you wherever you go" (Joshua 1:9).

Be specific. When we focus our prayers, we witness the faithfulness of God. Years ago, I had just finished a consulting contract and was looking for a new project. I had always wanted to write a book. I prayed, "Lord, if it is Your will, may it be so." A couple of weeks later, my husband called me from his office with the news that our denomination wanted us to write a book on second-career ministry.[20] That news and God's mercy blew me away!

Some folks keep a prayer journal, which is a neat way to list spiritual needs and add specific prayers. We are privileged to witness God's faithfulness as prayers are answered and burdens lifted.

Prayer connects us to God. We are blessed with a direct connection and the ability to ask Him to work in our lives to change things and change us (sometimes in ways we do not expect). It is a spiritual practice of adoration, confession, thankfulness, fulfillment, and petitions. It is a practice of renewal, growth, and direction. We can open our hearts and lives to His leading!

What do you pray for? What guidance is God giving you?

Spiritual Fruit

We've talked about spiritual anchoring, staying connected to God through the Word and the grace-filled ways God

---

20 Raymond and Martha Van Buskirk, *Leap of Faith: A Resource for Spirit-led Explorers* (St. Louis: Board for Pastoral Education of The Lutheran Church—Missouri Synod, 2009).

connects and empowers us: confession and absolution, Baptism, the Lord's Supper, the fellowship of other believers, and prayer. Sermons, books, podcasts, and other resources add spiritual help to our lives.

In the book of John, Jesus uses an agricultural analogy to explain what happens to our lives as we are spiritually connected to Him:

> **I am the true vine, and My Father is the vinedresser. Every branch in Me that does not bear fruit He takes away, and every branch that does bear fruit He prunes, that it may bear more fruit. Already you are clean because of the word that I have spoken to you. Abide in Me, and I in you. As the branch cannot bear fruit by itself, unless it abides in the vine, neither can you, unless you abide in Me. I am the vine; you are the branches. Whoever abides in Me and I in him, he it is that bears much fruit, for apart from Me you can do nothing. (John 15:1–5)**

Fruit is the result of our lives when we are connected to the vine that is the Lord. We are part of Him, and He of us. We grow, flourish, and provide fruit when empowered by the Holy Spirit, who inspires our faith actions, changing us. Evidence of fruit means we have visible godly actions, behavior, and growth, made possible by our spiritual connection to Jesus.

We will have spiritual ups and downs. Sometimes we will feel close to God, so connected. Other times we will feel distant. We may wonder if God is listening to our prayers, if He hears us, if He cares. He most certainly does: "Even the hairs of your head are all numbered" (Matthew 10:30), and "He hears us in whatever we ask" (1 John 5:15).

If we are distracted or busy and skip the spiritual filling, we create distance. We can feel isolated or overwhelmed. I find a correlation between my time spent in spiritual anchoring and the strength of my connection to the Lord. Is that your experience too?

Whatever challenges we face, we can know that we are not alone when anchored to our Lord. I love the way church planter and author Ted Doering encourages us to "abide" in the Lord:

> The promise of abiding is that those who do will bear fruit. The promise of justification is passive; you don't do anything! As Jesus keeps His promises in justification, He invites you to join in His work by abiding in Him, which contains a secondary promise: that you will bear fruit.[21]

For this blessing of spiritual fruit, we need to stay connected to the Vine, Jesus, as we remember our Baptism, partake in the Lord's Supper, read the Word, rest in His love, and marvel at how He covers us by His grace through repentance and forgiveness. In my own life, I seek to stay in the sweet, beautiful flow of the Holy Spirit as He works in and through me. My heart and soul are committed to and strengthened by Him, giving me hope, trust, and peace:

> Blessed is the man who trusts in the LORD, whose trust is the LORD. He is like a tree planted by water, that sends out its roots by the stream, and does not fear when heat comes, for its leaves remain green, and is not anxious in the year of drought, for it does not cease to bear fruit. (Jeremiah 17:7–8)

---

21 Ted Doering, *Walking Together: Simple Steps for Discipleship* (St. Louis: Concordia Publishing House, 2021), 34.

Lead me and show me, Lord. Let me be rooted in You so that I may abide in You and be a lively branch with fruit for You and Your glory!

POINTS TO PONDER (INDIVIDUALLY OR IN A SMALL GROUP, BOOK CLUB, OR BIBLE STUDY)

- How do you stay spiritually anchored? What gets you off track?

- How have you seen specific prayers work in your life and the lives of others?

- How have you seen your spiritual connection—your connection to the vine, Jesus—support you and provide fruit in your day-to-day life?

ACTION CHALLENGE

- Spend time today spiritually anchoring yourself through devotional and prayer time.

- Consider how much spiritual-filling time you spend; adjust as needed. Abide in the Lord and praise Him for the ways you are spiritually filled.

- Be thankful for spiritual fruit and ask God to lead you forward in His purpose.

PRAYER

Almighty Father, we praise and worship You. You are the one true God. Thank You for hearing our prayers and caring for us. Forgive us when we are distracted by the world in our busy lives. Thank You for Your Word and Sacraments. Thank You for Your forgiveness. We are grateful for Your gift of the Holy Spirit, who lives in us and guides us. Keep us close to You, anchored in Your Word. Fill us and guide us spiritually, so that in each step You shine in us and we bear fruit for Your kingdom. In the name of our Vine of life, Jesus. Amen.

CHAPTER 4
LIVING IN A FALLEN WORLD

BIBLICAL ANCHOR: JOHN 16:33

I have said these things to you, that in Me you may have peace. In the world you will have tribulation. But take heart; I have overcome the world.

KEY TAKEAWAY

Sometimes we think that because we're believers, we will skip life's troubles. Or we believe that God is too big to care about our individual trials. Not so—times two! In our times of suffering and crisis, which are inevitable, God is right there with us. Always. He promises to hold, comfort, and give us what we need for the hard steps of the journey—to never, ever leave us. How wonderful!

We've Got Trouble

In our fallen world, suffering is unavoidable. Sometimes people mistakenly believe that followers of Jesus are protected from all evil and won't have any problems. Scripture doesn't back that up: "Be sober-minded; be watchful. Your adversary the devil prowls around like a roaring lion, seeking someone to devour" (1 Peter 5:8).

Bad things can happen to anyone, and they do happen to everyone. Some folks seem to suffer more than others. But God is not the author of evil. Sin first entered the world in the

Garden of Eden, and evil is still alive and well today, causing great strife in our communities and world. Hate, conflict, persecution, and disaster are evidence that evil is everywhere.

If you watch the news or follow social media, you receive a full helping of this darkness each and every day. It can be discouraging, even depressing. (My advice? Limit screen news time and find balanced ways to be informed.)

But the fact remains: there is great darkness in the world. Bad things can and do happen to us and those we love.

The Suffering Is Real

What about the suffering that results from these hard times and hard things? Suffering is part of the believer's journey. We can explore different types:

- *Suffering caused by others:* We suffer because of the wrong of someone else, such as a driver who runs a red light and hits us, the seemingly innocuous link on our computer that seeks access to our accounts for fraudulent purposes, the harmful poisons that hurt our environment and our bodies where we live or work. (Basically, when others break the Ten Commandments and civil laws and engage in unethical behavior, we can suffer.)

- *Suffering we bring upon ourselves:* When we sin and reap the negative consequences, such as when we lie or gossip and lose the trust of others, when we aren't faithful to our spouse and damage the relationship, when we cheat on our taxes and get caught. (As we obey the Ten Commandments, we stay in God's safety zone of protection. When we break the rules, we bring pain to ourselves and others.)

- *Group-based natural suffering*: A natural disaster that has nothing personal to do with us but is devastating nonetheless, such as a tsunami, flood, fire, hurricane, drought, or earthquake. Because of sin, the natural world is broken. (As a Houstonian, I have witnessed our region experiencing crisis during hurricanes such as Harvey. We suffer just by living in a particular place. Some of you have endured similar circumstances.)

- *Group-based man-made suffering*: Large-scale suffering that originates with a human act and impacts an area or people or time in history, such as war, a purposefully or accidentally set forest fire, economic depression, or a pandemic. (Think of people whose lives are upended or ended by war, and how the world was impacted by the COVID-19 pandemic.)

- *Individual random suffering*: When our lives are changed negatively by something individually specific, such as cancer or other illness without an obvious cause, a freak accident, or something caused by others when we are caught up in the consequences, such as being a crime victim. (This type of suffering is especially challenging because we don't see a reason for it; it just happens, or we are at the wrong place at the wrong time.)

Suffering can take different forms: spiritual, mental, relational, social, physical, financial, and vocational. Sometimes, faithful disciples suffer persecution as a result of sharing their faith while serving as a light and witness in the world.

You might ask, Why even bring this up? I hear you. I bring this up because sometimes we think people who are positive or joyful don't have challenges in their lives. Or that to shine, we need to have a "perfect" life (not possible). In my experience, everyone has challenges, and these challenges are different for each of us.

On the other hand, sometimes believers embrace toxic positivity, thinking it's necessary to always be positive and cheerful to prove faithfulness in the Lord. We can refuse to recognize or address our negative emotions or the experiences of others, denying reality and the need for help. In doing so, we can prevent ourselves or others from seeking care: God's healing prayer, therapies, counseling, medicines, and other remedies.

Case in point: A church member shared a terrible personal health situation, then smiled with forced brightness, "God is good all the time." Yes, God is good all the time. But sometimes, life is tough, and it's not a lack of faith to say so.

When we acknowledge struggle, we are being honest with ourselves and others. We open ourselves to receiving kindness and help from others and the Lord. We can say, "This [challenge] is tough, painful. It's hard to be positive. But I know God is faithful. He is with me each day and will see me through this tough situation."

My husband's first pastoral call took us from our preseminary home in the Washington, DC, area to an industrial city in southeast Texas. The location was a 180-degree turn in terms of geography and culture. It was tough to come into a smaller community where most people who lived there had grown up there. Living as outsiders brought certain kinds of hardship and suffering.

People didn't know about my status jobs in DC and didn't care. A painful and beneficial process began. I began to lose my preoccupation with earthly "identities," mostly status-related possessions and achievements I believed gave me worth. A spiritual sloughing-off scoured me back to my core identity and worth as a child of God. (Whew! I can write that easily enough here, but it was a journey.)

Today, I know that I am worthy of God's love, and I dearly hope you know that you are worthy of God's love, whatever our status and possessions and job. Whoever we are, we are worthy of carrying out His purposes. I don't need to rely on status indicators to determine my value. I have inherent value as a creation of the King, His heir by the water and Word of my Baptism. There's nothing I have to do or achieve to be loved by Him. In His eyes, and through the redemptive sacrifice of Jesus, I am enough.

Although much progress has been made—thanks to God and an excellent therapist—I still struggle with pride and indications of worth. In God's beautiful teaching way, as He leads me toward my better, more sanctified self, He lovingly reminds me that His love extends to all people. Not just the "important" people. He doesn't love "successful" people more; in fact, we see in the Bible how God's heart is especially drawn to the poor and needy in body, soul, and mind.

Despite the difficulty of the situation, God orchestrated significant ministry experiences and lessons during our service at that congregation. My husband faithfully led a Word-and-Sacrament ministry. Our congregation survived demographic changes. A Spanish-speaking companion congregation was launched, and it is still active today. God provided specific help for me in the journey; I can see that now. The placement there was challenging, but it served as a staging area for my needed spiritual growth.

Other times, suffering is tragic, plain and simple. We can acknowledge the pain and call upon our heavenly Father for help. He is always there: "Fear not, for I am with you; be not dismayed, for I am your God; I will strengthen you, I will help you, I will uphold you with My righteous right hand" (Isaiah 41:10). While we may gather some threads of joy or provision during a painful time, it's a terrible situation and our hearts cry out to God for help.

In our challenges, sometimes it's easy to linger and get swallowed up by the struggles. But we can hold fast to God. If we are feeling discouraged, outside assistance may be just the thing to help with the overwhelming situation. We can talk with a pastor and work with a therapist, someone to come alongside and help us get unstuck and back to hope. We can also reach out to trusted friends and family to lend a hand when and where possible. We don't need to hesitate to ask.

We continue to pray. We struggle, and sometimes even battle, to hang on to hope. We ask people to pray for us. God will give His spiritual comfort and power even as we communicate our needs to Him—He is already aware of what we need, even before we are. We often see God's help in response to prayer, in both the short and long term. (I've seen beautiful answers after days, weeks, months, and even years of prayer.)

Other times, we continue to suffer but experience a positive though unexpected development. Or our hearts are changed by God, and we pray in a new way. Sometimes, we need or receive different answers. In response to prayer, God may even allow us to witness miraculous healing or experience blessed moments—or not (see 2 Corinthians 12:8–9).

We also know that sometimes, despite our faith and fervent prayer and hope, a tough situation doesn't go away. Our dear aunt loses her battle with cancer. We continue to experience financial troubles or relationship heartbreak. A natural disaster hits our region and brings devastation, even though we prayed it wouldn't. This is the reality of living in a fallen world. Bad things still happen, but God is still with us. His Spirit gets us through tough times.

Here's the point: Folks who shine don't shine because they don't have troubles. They shine because their hearts are anchored in the Lord. In this anchoring, we experience His love and care and faithfulness through the suffering—through the good *and* the bad.

When we are anchored in Him, Jesus shines in us and through us by the Holy Spirit. God is right there with us, always—despite what the world throws at us!

Remember the Promises

As the apostle Paul shares in Romans 12:12, "Rejoice in hope, be patient in tribulation, be constant in prayer." We might say, "Rejoice? What's happening to me or my loved one is really awful!" Sometimes it is. But we can hold fast to hope because of two core truths:

1. Jesus overcame the power of the devil through His sacrificial death and resurrection, providing salvation and victory for those who believe in Him. We are good for our forever future.

2. God is always, always there for us. It is impossible for us
   to go outside of His interest or care. He is trustworthy
   to hold us in His hands and to strengthen us, no matter
   what happens. He sends His Spirit to comfort and guide
   our hearts.

We can count on Jesus, our Savior. He is faithful. My friend Rev. Wayne Graumann shares that when times are especially tough, we can simply *fall* into Jesus' grace and mercy. (Love this!) Whatever it is. No matter what. We can pray for protection, provision, and healing. Above all, we can call upon Jesus' name for help and receive His peace.

Sometimes, though, because we live in a sinful world, we don't get the outcome we hoped for. Regardless of what happens, faith brings comfort and strength through the challenges. As author, speaker, and podcaster Michelle Diercks shares: "The peace of God's presence gives us hope in uncertainty, strength for each moment, and the ability to persevere through trials. His presence provides a place for our souls to rest in who He is as our loving Creator."[22] Amen!

God's Got You

You can lean into God and rest in His loving care, "casting all your anxieties on Him, because He cares for you" (1 Peter 5:7).

The apostle Paul adds: "Not only that, but we rejoice in our sufferings, knowing that suffering produces endurance, and endurance produces character, and character produces hope,

---

22 Michelle Diercks, *Promised Rest: Finding Peace in God's Presence* (St. Louis: Concordia Publishing House, 2022), 9.

and hope does not put us to shame, because God's love has been poured into our hearts through the Holy Spirit who has been given to us" (Romans 5:3–5).

Does that mean we're joyful and jump up and down when bad things happen to us and the ones we love? By no means! The good news: the Bible assures us that no matter what happens, God is there with us—always—and promises to bring something good out of it. It might be insight, a restored relationship, new wisdom, or humility; with our God, the possibilities are endless. Keep an eye out.

Trouble is inevitable. God in His mercy can bring something good out of our trials: "Beloved, do not be surprised at the fiery trial when it comes upon you to test you, as though something strange were happening to you. But rejoice insofar as you share Christ's sufferings, that you may also rejoice and be glad when His glory is revealed" (1 Peter 4:12–13).

God won the victory. As author, speaker, and Bible teacher Donna Snow reminds us, "No matter what life brings today, we know how this story ends. Who wins. Who conquered the grave. Who conquered sin in our place. And because of that we can walk in complete confidence today. Not in our strength, His. Without any fear."[23]

We can expect joy and also challenges and suffering along life's way. Stuff happens. Despite the troubles of the world, God is with us in each and every step. Through faith in Jesus, our Savior, our forever-home is set. Although life can be tough, by the faith that the Holy Spirit works in us, we can be anchored and strengthened, shining because of Jesus' light in us!

---

23 Donna Snow, Facebook, November 7, 2022, https://www.facebook.com /donna.snow.67/posts/pfbid0Lgt8A7p8pnGGfZjGRj8eGLjaiUay71FNzE3 GzAvgf2yHMoY4wcHgX2WwrPNUnHqol.

POINTS TO PONDER (INDIVIDUALLY OR IN A SMALL GROUP, BOOK CLUB, OR BIBLE STUDY)

- What is challenging you today? What support do you need today?

- How have you seen God's faithfulness throughout life's troubles?

- What has God taught you in your struggles? How has He given you hope? joy?

ACTION CHALLENGE

- Remember a time when God got you through a tough situation, and thank Him once again.

- Pray for strength to deal with life's challenges and remain a faithful witness. Pray for someone who is suffering now.

- Thank God for being with you, no matter what. Read Bible verses to remind you of His love, faithfulness, and care.

PRAYER

Father in heaven, our almighty Creator, You are faithful and trustworthy. You know our hearts and situations. Forgive us when we worry and doubt Your great love for us. In this world we will have trouble. Thank You for always, always hearing our prayers. We ask for the powerful help and guidance of Your Spirit through the ever-present challenges of life. Help us to see Your goodness and provision even in tough circumstances. Help us to shine even as we struggle. In the name of Jesus. Amen.

CHAPTER 5
WORSHIP AND THE GREAT BEYOND

BIBLICAL ANCHOR: ACTS 2:46-47

And day by day, attending the temple together and breaking bread in their homes, they received their food with glad and generous hearts, praising God and having favor with all the people. And the Lord added to their number day by day those who were being saved.

KEY TAKEAWAY

Worship and fellowship with other believers are essential to our Christian walk. We praise the triune God. We are built up by our brothers and sisters in Christ and grow in our knowledge of the Lord and our service to Him. Thank God for the church! Sometimes, though, we can become overly insular and comfortable in our beloved church homes. Led and powered by the Holy Spirit, let's continue to step forward and share the light of Christ in new and outward-reaching ways.

Essential Worship

Worship is foundational to our faith and our primary church purpose. It's a natural response to God's creation, Jesus' sacrifice on the cross for our sins, and Christ's gift of redemptive salvation.

As the Body of Christ—Jesus' followers throughout the world—we gather together in our churches. We anchor ourselves to the Rock of Ages, receiving God's grace through His Word, the Lord's Supper, and Baptism. We also receive the benefits of fellowship among other believers. We can thank and praise God as we are strengthened and filled, forgiven and forgiving. We support others and are supported.

In this collective spiritual time, we encourage one another. We pray for one another and for our neighbors, community, country, and world. We are fortified by singing hymns and songs. We hear the Word and are spiritually fed by it; we receive the Lord's Supper and are sustained in faith. We study the Bible together and deepen our understanding as God works through His living Word. We listen to the pastor's sermon, reflecting on the message and its application in our lives. In attending the Divine Service, we grow in our knowledge of the Lord, and we are strengthened in our faith walk.

I love this time with my brothers and sisters in Christ, and I'm grateful for the uplift from the Holy Spirit and the support, prayer, and affirmation from fellow church members. We can feel the power of the Spirit as hearts gather in the Lord's name, dedicated to His purposes: "For where two or three are gathered in My name, there am I among them" (Matthew 18:20).

The church is our earthly spiritual gathering place. In addition to worship and Bible study, we experience landmark rites of life: Baptism, confirmation in the faith, weddings, and funerals. And in our attendance, we grow, belong, and serve. I love my church, one of God's glory-filled filling stations!

Church Service

In addition to worship, many of us volunteer or work at our churches as we are able. Perhaps we serve as a teacher or other called church worker. We might volunteer to sing in the choir, help with a ministry to children, support the altar guild, manage financial systems, or lead assistance ministries. There are so many wonderful ways to serve!

The church is God's vehicle to build His kingdom and help others grow in faith and service to Him. Something special happens when we gather with our brothers and sisters in praise and thanksgiving. God works through people. In connection to others, we can serve as conduits for His purposes. We gather together with other individuals, families, groups, and congregations to learn His will.

Churches do mission work among their members, in their neighborhood, and around the world. Therefore, it is important to bless our churches with our time, talents, and treasure. Such support helps our churches to be places where people can find resources for their spiritual walk. By sharing our gifts, churches can provide inspiration from God for those who need it, including ourselves and fellow believers, giving encouragement in both good and bad times.

Some of us have had negative experiences with a church. My dad was a pastor and, even as an elementary school–aged child, I remember seeing someone at church and thinking, "That person doesn't like my daddy." (I'm thankful that I also witnessed many expressions of Christian love and care from church members over the years.) You may have experienced internal church fights, gossip, attacks on the pastor, and conflict among members.

In this fallen world, every one of us is a sinner. Therefore, every church is led by and filled with sinners. Let's rely on God to keep His light within us and guide us in love and discernment, confession and absolution, forgiveness and reconciliation. "This is the message we have heard from Him and proclaim to you, that God is light, and in Him is no darkness at all" (1 John 1:5).

Please don't allow the mistakes, unkindnesses, unforgiveness, or hypocrisy of people in your congregation keep you from being close to Jesus and experiencing a full and vibrant spiritual life. Work to prayerfully and peacefully resolve differences in your church and between church members. Anchor in His Word and seek the wisdom of the Holy Spirit to guide you. Please seek additional spiritual help if you are having trouble getting past a negative experience.

Likewise, lean on God in prayer when you are tempted to sin in your church setting. Stay away from gossip and triangulation, such as when someone shares an issue he or she is having with someone else instead of working it out with that person directly. If you disagree with someone or something, follow the wise precepts of Matthew 18:15–20 in conflict resolution. Forgive and be forgiven. Pray for strength, wisdom, and discernment.

Let's keep kindness at the forefront of our church membership and not insist on everything our own way. The pastor is working not only for the good of us individually but also for everyone in the congregation collectively. Answers or policies may be different than we expect. Let's give and receive a generous measure of God's grace as we worship and work with our pastors and fellow church members.

And if you volunteer at your church—whether you prepare the Lord's Supper for the service, support mission efforts, greet visitors, or teach a Bible class—know that all jobs in our churches are important and make a difference in God's kingdom. Thank you!

Some folks are already filled to the brim with purpose as they serve in their vocations through the daily care of others. These souls are grateful just to get to church. And some have challenges of their own and are thrilled to physically attend services, to be welcomed and fed and fortified for life in this challenging world. Welcome these people; it is an honor to serve those who serve others and those who aren't physically able to serve in most ways.

Let's embrace good self-care and good boundaries as we serve in our church and beyond. As Christians, we are not obligated to say yes to every request, and we are not obligated to say yes to unreasonable requests. Although sometimes we help when help is needed, we serve best when we serve in our unique callings, practicing discernment and matching the needs of our church with our own divinely given talents.

My husband has never been and never will be a youth pastor. But get him around older adults or young children, and he's amazing. His gifts are just right for serving these special populations. Others have different gifts and areas of focus. My love is welcoming others and building relationships at church. My mom loves her ladies' missionary group and helping with the monthly luncheon for veterans at her church. These ministry places are well-matched for each of us.

In that first congregation, God gave my husband specific leadership purposes as pastor. God also led me to a unique and needed way to serve that filled a gap. There was no choir or special music when we began. Together with two church members and our three kids, we formed a music group. We sang every week, sharing beautiful hymns and new songs. It was collegial, positive, and spiritually encouraging. We stepped in to fill a congregational need, led by a "nudge" (thanks, Holy Spirit!)

and an interest to serve in this way. God provided the musical gifts. What a blessing!

You may already be serving, or you may have a special challenge that limits your participation. Take care and be reasonable, friend. Constant care of children or another family member, for example, is spiritual work that is often undervalued but expends a great deal of effort and energy for a season. As you receive requests for service, graciously consider each one with prayer, asking God to lead you with His wisdom. Caring for oneself sometimes means opting out of activities for the greater benefit.

I used to work in politics, where the work always involved trying to increase the number of people in leadership by bringing in new folks and giving each person something to do. In our churches, we can look to include others, praying for guidance to work wisely and match our church needs and requests with what fits each individual and his or her God-given talents and interests. At one of our churches, the pastors prayed over the membership list each year, seeking guidance on encouraging members to individual, specific service.

We can overdo it when we always step in to serve. We can neglect self-care and even prevent others from serving, leading, or developing their gifts. We don't have to do everything; as the saying goes, let's be instruments of God's peace, not the whole orchestra.

For some of us, this means working toward a balanced, healthy level of service. Sometimes that means saying no to something good. Saying no doesn't mean you're not a good Christian. Rely on God to lead you to the right places for your service, and also to tenderly rest and care for your spiritual health and physical body—your temple. May good self-care be a priority, and may you be led to just the right places for your light to shine.

Whatever the situation, God's people gather at church to worship and serve in their vocations as they are able. (If you've stepped out of church attendance and haven't yet stepped back in, take a step forward and worship this Sunday.) It's a place for us to gather and be strengthened, which is essential in today's tough times.

> **Now to Him who is able to do far more abundantly than all that we ask or think, according to the power at work within us, to Him be glory in the church and in Christ Jesus throughout all generations, forever and ever. Amen.** (Ephesians 3:20–21)

Out and About

Gathering at church is a strong way to connect to the light of Christ, who shines in us by the presence of the Holy Spirit within us. We shine His light when we are filled in this way: "In the same way, let your light shine before others, so that they may see your good works and give glory to your Father who is in heaven" (Matthew 5:16).

As we live our daily lives, we can also "walk out" our faith and shine because of what He has done in us. (Yay! And thank You!)

The Holy Spirit is our life-cycle leader, welcoming us, making us holy, sanctifying us. Creating faith in our hearts at our Baptism, the Spirit gives us strength for the every day, confirms our belonging, and illuminates the way forward in our Christian walk through continued spiritual growth. We trust our sure future in heaven.

It's a beautiful, comforting experience as we regularly anchor ourselves through the Word and Sacrament and share our hearts through worship and prayer. The Holy Spirit works within us to encourage, teach, and inspire. He can give us a loving nudge when we do something selfish or unkind, saying, "Did you notice it? With My help, you can do better." Or He can encourage us to go forward, showing the way and saying, "Why don't you [insert kind deed here]?"

Strengthened by the means of grace, our thankful and sanctified hearts outwardly express our faith through words and deeds. Through the Spirit, we are powered up to shine. Not perfectly, but willingly, we serve the Lord with gladness (see Psalm 100:2). We rely on Him to set our course, show the way, and provide the power and wisdom for the journey. We ask Him to show us the folks He wants us to reach and to lead our work step by step.

And where to, beyond church? We may have a small or large amount of time and energy to share. As we see throughout the New Testament, Jesus focused on teaching His disciples and reaching outsiders in His earthly ministry. Our Lord cherished connections with those struggling and in need of the one true light: known sinners, the lost, vulnerable, outcast, or unpopular folks He encountered on the way. The kind of folks you will also encounter.

Let us consider our daily paths. How can we better shine the light of Jesus in our household, to our neighbors, and to those around us? To the people we encounter in our daily walk, our pathways? In our individual lives, we are placed in a certain space and time. God can use us wherever we go, even to the grocery store or in conversation with our next-door neighbor! (We can even be kinder to ourselves, right?)

Worship anchors us in our faith. With fresh eyes, with mercy, let's look to those we can serve in the first circles outside our church homes—the nearby mission field. We pray for God's direction, knowing He will guide us for His purposes: "Let the favor of the Lord our God be upon us, and establish the work of our hands upon us; yes, establish the work of our hands!" (Psalm 90:17).

POINTS TO PONDER (INDIVIDUALLY OR IN A SMALL GROUP, BOOK CLUB, OR BIBLE STUDY)

- What are your favorite parts of worship and church activities?

- How can you ask for help or serve both inside and outside your church?

- In what ways do you reserve time for spiritual self-care, balancing your service to the Lord with time for devotional anchoring and the guidance of the Holy Spirit?

ACTION CHALLENGE

- Thank God for your church. (If you don't yet have a church home, begin your search. Pray for Him to lead you to the congregation that is right for you.)

- Take an inventory of how you are helping at your church. How does your service reflect your unique spiritual gifts and experiences? Where do you need to say yes? Where do you need to say no? Is there something you've always wanted to do? Pray, and take an exploratory step.

- Ask God to show you where He wants you to serve, either in the same ways or in new ways. Listen for His guidance.

PRAYER

Holy Father, we worship You. We praise You. We thank You for Your church here on earth, our spiritual home where we gather, learn, and worship You alongside our brothers and sisters in Christ. Forgive us when we become too cozy and comfortable in our church homes and neglect the mission field. Guide our work. Use our gifts. Lead our congregations. May we serve You in gladness and in the ways You lead us to shine, inside and out. We pray this in the name of Your one true light, Your Son, Jesus. Amen.

CHAPTER 6
HEALTHY HELPING

BIBLICAL ANCHOR: EPHESIANS 4:1–2

I therefore, a prisoner for the Lord, urge you to walk in a manner worthy of the calling to which you have been called, with all humility and gentleness, with patience, bearing with one another in love.

KEY TAKEAWAY

As we seek to help others in the name of Christ, we can follow best practices and help others in healthy ways, spiritually and relationally. We can skip the judgment, assumptions, and other limiting mindsets. We can be open to the beautiful diversity of people, experiences, and situations where we can make a difference, guided by the light, Jesus.

Humble Beginnings

My writing career has been cause-driven, focusing primarily on nonprofits, that is, organizations that provide help to others. I've seen helps created and provided in many ways, and share a few best practices, supported by Scripture, to assist in our loving service.

Begin with humility and compassion. Remember that our Lord came down from heaven and took on human form, served others unto death, sacrificing Himself for us:

Who, though He was in the form of God, did not count equality with God a thing to be grasped, but emptied

Himself, by taking the form of a servant, being born in the likeness of men. And being found in human form, He humbled Himself by becoming obedient to the point of death, even death on a cross. (Philippians 2:6–8)

The Gospel calls us to faith. Christ's sacrifice was complete, and thus our salvation and future were assured. There's nothing we can do or have to do in order to receive this incredible gift. His grace—unmerited favor—is given to us and received by that same faith. Not because we are good or smart or super helpful. Just because we are His. His love makes us accepted, forgiven, and free. Then, God calls us to serve others:

What good is it, my brothers, if someone says he has faith but does not have works? Can that faith save him? If a brother or sister is poorly clothed and lacking in daily food, and one of you says to them, "Go in peace, be warmed and filled," without giving them the things needed for the body, what good is that? So also faith by itself, if it does not have works, is dead. (James 2:14–17)

It's a both-and situation, meaning we are saved freely by God's grace and we are called to do good works. Service to others is part of the expression of our faith life. In a divine way, the Holy Spirit provides opportunities for us to serve His purposes in the places we live, work, volunteer, worship, and travel every day. God delivers opportunities to us, right where we are.

Down and Out

Skip the judgment. I'm sad to admit this, but I've judged others harshly. Many times. Passing judgment on someone else makes me feel better about myself, especially in areas where I see myself as lacking. It seems to give me an excuse not to help or witness to that person. This is not God's way. Judgment is not our job; it's His:

> **Judge not, that you be not judged.** (Matthew 7:1)

> **There is only one lawgiver and judge, He who is able to save and to destroy. But who are you to judge your neighbor?** (James 4:12)

Jesus provides heavenly inspiration for us to look around with new eyes, ready to follow His lead and serve His purposes. As we've explored in Scripture, our Lord's loving gaze often looked beyond status stations of the day to unexpected people. As our Lord and Savior-to-be, during His time on earth, He was open to anyone and everyone.

Remember these folks from our Bible stories:

- Woman caught in adultery (women in that culture were low status; she was also a known sinner), John 8:2–11

- Children (low status), Matthew 19:14

- Beggar who was blind (believed to be blind because of sin), Luke 18:35–43

- Roman centurion (hated oppressor and outsider), Luke 7:1–10

We can reflect on Jesus' actions as He lived and traveled among us all those years ago. Not only did Jesus teach but He also leaned in to help those who were needy, very young, sick, spiritually lost, and beggars. He was open to a centurion, a tax collector, a man who had leprosy. This is an active, upside-down approach! Despite His godly and coequal place with the Father and Holy Spirit, our Savior saw people who were lost and "had compassion on them" (Matthew 14:14). Wow!

It's good to remember that we're all in need of help in some way. Poverty can be poorness in mind or soul, not just financial need. It is easy to assume that just because someone is wealthy, that person is "good"; or that because someone is poor, that person doesn't have good values or isn't working hard. But our possessions and jobs don't make us worthy of respect and love. We all have value because we were created by our loving Father. We are worthy of love, and we are precious to Him; we are all deserving of His notice.

Even with ample resources and freedom, we can be the needy ones, not living out our full potential but instead leading self-focused lives, shallow and insular. I feel that way sometimes about my own life.

Let's join Jesus in His upside-down ministry. Let's skip our assumptions, which can be faulty. God's rich gifting applies to all His human creations, and we are all worthy of His attention.

Judging and condemning others closes our heart to compassion. Yet compassion is most often the just-right response. What can we do with our own small lives to help, to ease, to encourage? How can we, through the guidance and power of the Holy Spirit, bring the light of the Gospel into situations?

Jesus' ministry was accomplished in this town and that, with this group and that person. Wherever He went. Sometimes among those with high status, but most often among those of low status. In our own very human and imperfect way, we too can zoom in and serve the "world" right where we are. Our objective in serving is to demonstrate the love of Jesus through our words and actions, opening the door to the Gospel. We can hope and wait expectantly to see where the Spirit leads!

How Can I Serve You?

In our bustling, busy society, the suffering of others can often be the result of a shortage of time, attention, resources, or opportunity. They (and we) can be lonely and depressed. Perhaps someone is just making ends meet and feels overwhelmed. Maybe they're concerned about health, safety, old age, or the next meal. The pandemic and world unrest have only added to our challenges, anxieties, and fears.

It's true that we can't personally stop wars or save nations. But what if we simply start where we are, in our own footprint, and serve the Lord with fresh eyes and ears? Not big and conspicuous, but small and ordinary. Let's skip the bluster and the showcasing of benevolence to show how "great" we are. Let's keep our method quiet but active.

So who's there? A neighbor lives alone and has no family nearby. A forgotten relative whom we avoid because the situation makes us uncomfortable. The single-mom grocery clerk who's just trying to make ends meet and feels the world closing in on her from all sides. The elderly man who feels forgotten and unappreciated. The anxious young person in our family who is growing up in a turbulent world full of conflict and uncertainty.

Because of extremely rapid change in our society, young people and elders are living vastly different lives from one another. Many of us are pedaling as fast as we can to stay updated and relevant in today's world. Or we give up, unable to keep up. We accept our limitations, meanwhile longing for days past when the world seemed a little nicer and not so crazy.

Whether near or far, inside or outside of our own families, opportunities exist for us to shine the light of Christ with our crotchety uncle, an aging parent, a nephew we don't understand, or an adult child we can't seem to get along with. These opportunities go into and beyond our immediate family as we venture out into the next circles of our daily lives. We can listen. We can seek to understand. We can follow the wise instructions that our Lord gave to the people of Israel:

> **When you reap your harvest in your field and forget a sheaf in the field, you shall not go back to get it. It shall be for the sojourner, the fatherless, and the widow, that the LORD your God may bless you in all the work of your hands. (Deuteronomy 24:19)**

You may already be there, praying constantly as you work to connect or repair. Don't give up. We can embrace and share once again the soft and lovely light of Christ with those right around us, revealing His love through our words and actions.

Healthy Basics

What does healthy help look like? So often, I've jumped in and tried to fix things: "Wonderful me is going to solve this problem beautifully and in a snap." This is embarrassing to share, but it's true. Don't get me wrong: leadership and organization skills are good gifts. Yet sometimes we don't know the context or backstory of another person's circumstances. We can be in a rush to "remedy" that person's situation and do not take time to gather the facts or receive permission to engage in the situation.

Additionally, most of us have been raised to believe that help is always, well, helpful. When I go to help my ninety-one-year-old mom with something she doesn't need help with, it's patronizing. When I push my agenda at a family party, I overlook that it's not my event but a celebration by and for someone else. This brings to mind the term "inflicting kindness."

(About that party: I had to step back, have a talk with myself—which was hard when I was so full of good ideas— and say to the hostess, "How would you like me to help?" and then proceed to help in that way, not mine. You get the picture, right?)

When we step in to help from our perspective and without checking in, when we try to solve things our way instead of the way that would be the most valuable to the person being helped or the way he or she wants to be helped, we can fail at being actually helpful.

Here are a few guidelines:

Help is permission-based. All people have the right to say yes or no. When we see someone on a scooter at the grocery store, struggling to get an item out of the frozen section, we can say, "Hey, would you like some help with that?" And the struggler can say, "Yes, please," or, "No, I've got it."

If the answer is no, we respect the person's decline with a smile and go on our way. We do not inflict kindness by going on to say, for example, "Oh, it's no trouble. I'll get it for you right now," and push through to grab the item despite the person's wish for self-reliance.

If the answer is yes, we also can skip the sad face that says, "Oh, you poor dear." People usually don't want pity. They're doing their best and are determined to do what they can.

I have an older neighbor who lives alone. I rarely see this neighbor, but when we had a power outage, I had a rare opportunity to greet her outside and start a conversation. It was a chance for me to connect, to ask, "Would it be okay if we exchanged phone numbers?" and "Will you please reach out to me if you need anything?" She said yes, and we took a baby step forward in our relationship. I was also able to share the power outage map link she was looking for and was delighted to have.

Help people how they want to be helped. I still remember the basics from missions training years ago, when a group went into a community and decided to create a mission project without asking local people about their needs. Once completed, the project was rarely used. There's a saying in the nonprofit world: "Not for us without us," meaning, don't create helps for people without their involvement and direction. Makes sense, right?

My husband and I have come up with questions to ask in our interactions with my mom: Would you like us to go with you? Would you like us to drive you there or would you like to drive yourself? Would you like us to go into the doctor's office with you and take notes or stay in the waiting room? We ask; she decides.

Help often doesn't involve money or resources. For instance, listening is a wonderful way to serve. Sometimes when I'm discussing a challenge with my husband, he's all ideas and solutions, but I'm just brainstorming, so my response to him is "Sounds terrific, but what I need right now is your loving, listening ears. Thank you." That's hard for him because he loves me and is a smart one. But sometimes, all I need is someone to listen. Said another way, pay attention to the details of the discussion and ask clarifying questions.

Think about those who can use a little listening to. Maybe this is someone close to you or an acquaintance. Either way, perk up your ears!

Our experience is not their experience. Whatever the difference, it's a difference. If we've never been poor, we can't know how it feels. If we're not a person of color, we can't fully understand the experience. If we've never suffered from diabetes, cancer, anxiety, or COPD, we just can't know what it's like.

Vocations also present differences: if we aren't a military veteran, teacher, pastor, firefighter, nurse, or first-generation college student, we don't know what it's like. Even family members have differences. The perspectives of a grandmother and granddaughter will be different, based on generational placement and life experiences.

Ask, listen, learn, and be guided by the person you are talking with and by the promptings of the Holy Spirit. It is not possible to know what the lives of others are like. Keep in mind that the "good old days" weren't good for everyone. Even today, with all our prosperity and options, many people struggle with a lack of opportunity and understanding.

Good manners are for everyone, everywhere. We know the essentials: "Please" and "Thank you" and "How are you?" We can use such courteous language wherever we go. We can maintain our civility even in challenging situations or disagreements. From good waiting-in-line manners, group manners, and customer-service conversations, modern situations abound where we can shine and be a kindly presence out in the world. We can remember to say "Excuse me" as we pass through crowds or want to ask a question. We can open the door and let another person go ahead of us.

In our daily journeys, let's make eye contact, say hello, and ask people how they're doing, using a kind tone of voice. Give a smile and greeting. Be willing to wait a minute, to be patient with one another, even as we sometimes require the patience of others.

A personal favorite of mine is an immediate sharing of sincere appreciation. Whether it's expressed to our spouse, pastor, restaurant wait staff, or someone else who helps us, especially when that person goes above and beyond, let's share sincere and specific praise. (Can you think of a time when someone thanked you with specific details for something you did to help?) We benefit from the actions of others. Sharing specific compliments is returning the favor and is most welcome!

All people are in need, and all people are valued by God. Social status does not determine inherent value. Every person is equally valued by our Creator and gifted with specific talents. I don't have more value than others because I was born in the United States and have had great opportunities here.

The only hierarchy I can see in the Bible is when God gave humans dominion over the earth and all creatures and plants living in it (Genesis 1:26). Yep, that's it!

When we literally and figuratively put up our arms to block others who are different than us in some way, we close that relationship. There's no dialogue or shared learning, no compassion or mercy. The Gospel door is closed. Led by the Lord and relying on the Spirit, we can do better.

The beauty of actual help. How many times have I been nicey-nice but not actually helpful? This attitude of "sweet" but not helpful reminds me of the Texas saying "All hat and no cattle." I don't want to be this way; instead, I want to bolster my kind words with kind actions and sincerity. (Lord, help me to be both kind *and* helpful!)

A friend once shared an approach to support this thought. She recommended that instead of saying, "Let me know if you need anything," it is better to ask, "How can I help?" Even the simple act of dropping off a meal to a struggling family or sharing a meal with a lonely friend can be a lovely lift. A right-there help is offering to pray for someone or the person's situation: "May I pray for you now? What should we pray for?" And then actually pray aloud with that person, then and there.

A note to those in need: accepting help is not a weakness. Allow others the joy of serving you. When a friend was going through a challenging time, my husband and I offered to drop off a meal. My friend later told me she almost said no but was glad she accepted the offer. We were all blessed by it!

Those around us in our suffering world can be blessed by Jesus' light as it shines through us in healthy and divinely guided ways. Every time we leave our house, God shows us people we can let His light shine on. Remember, the little things are big things. Let's not hide our light under a bushel; instead, let us shine away as we serve God's purposes!

POINTS TO PONDER (INDIVIDUALLY OR IN A SMALL GROUP, BOOK CLUB, OR BIBLE STUDY)

- How has this chapter helped you to think differently about valuing and helping others?

- What do you think about the idea of "healthy help" versus "inflicting kindness"?

- Can you share healthy ways you've helped others and/or new ways you've considered to shine?

ACTION CHALLENGE

- Take steps to begin a habit of helping others by asking, "What can I do for you today?"

- Help someone this week in a way that does not involve money.

- Ask God to help you really see the people around you and to lead you to opportunities to shine.

PRAYER

Our dear heavenly Father, You are the author of all good things. You sent Your Son, Jesus, to save us and Your Spirit to daily help us. Forgive our lack of help or unhealthy ways of helping. Thank You for loving us and making us an important part of Your mission on earth. As we serve You, show us how You want us to be helpful. Lead us in healthy ways to value, respect, and serve others in the name of our Redeemer, Jesus. Amen.

CHAPTER 7
WE ARE FAMILY

BIBLICAL ANCHOR: 1 CORINTHIANS 13:4–7

Love is patient and kind; love does not envy or boast; it is not arrogant or rude. It does not insist on its own way; it is not irritable or resentful; it does not rejoice at wrongdoing, but rejoices with the truth. Love bears all things, believes all things, hopes all things, endures all things.

KEY TAKEAWAY

Our family is the first circle of ministry—the people God has placed closest to us—and can sometimes be the most difficult. Great purpose resides there! We can evade or "step over" tough relationships close at hand, missing service and growth opportunities in our own lives and with our own families. Let's begin with ourselves, at the beginning, and be open to forgiveness and embracing differences. May we practice sacrificial love like Jesus and get help when we're stuck.

Home Sweet Home

Rich opportunities to shine often reside in our homes. You may think, as I did, "I'm already kind to those around me!" And to be clear, this isn't some sort of caring contest. It's a sweet time to look around with new eyes and take a little inventory.

The Spirit has been working on me here. To be a bit gentler. Kinder. To thank those in my home for the daily things they do for me and for the rest of our family: chores, thoughtful errands and actions, meal preparation—the little ways we work together as a family team.

You might interject, "But we're supposed to do these things. We don't need to be thanked." Maybe. But give specific thanks a try. Nonverbal thanks can also be just the thing: a hug, a pat on the shoulder. Not overly done, just sharing appreciation and shining the light of Jesus in gratitude for the many kindnesses others do for us in our homes. Here are some places where thankfulness can shine:

- *With the chores.* We can live as more generous housemates. When a miracle happens and I vacuum, there's a temptation to skip my mother's apartment, which is part of our house. My thoughts go like this: "Oh, she doesn't really need her floors vacuumed today; I have so much going on and don't have the time; I can do it next time." Step back, selfishness! It takes five minutes, and Mom is thrilled.

- *Others first.* Perhaps you're easygoing and it doesn't really matter when decisions come up in your home; you're good with whatever. (Would you please join my family? I can be so particular and could use some balance.) With awareness and prayer, I'm becoming more flexible. Let's ensure that everyone gets a turn leading the prayer, choosing the movie, going first when sharing the news of the day, or having the last piece of pie.

- *Noticing.* When those we live with are distant, sad, elated, or tired, let's notice and respond. Take notice when someone gets lab results from the doctor but doesn't say anything. Pay attention to when "the day," *that* anniversary, comes around and the memories sadden. Celebrate when someone receives good news. When we pay attention to the ups and downs, we can gently open the conversation and create a connection, affirming for others that someone cares.

- *Taking time to listen.* We may not be listening enough to those in our own homes, to those closest to us. There can be so much going on in our lives that we focus on ourselves. It takes time and patience to really listen, to ask thoughtful questions, and to gently turn the conversation to the other person. Instead of reporting and retreating, we can ease the conversation along, building a dialogue where both or all engage. It takes time.

Especially as our family members age, we can be compassionate listeners to loved ones as they once again share a memory, a detailed symptom, a new diagnosis, or other worries about the world. Sometimes people simply want to recount and process a sickness, procedure, fear, or challenge. Our response, coming from a place of compassion, familiarity, and love, is to listen with a kind, receptive heart. And whether with our loved one or by ourselves, we can pray for one another.

If you live alone and you're Team You, give yourself a pat on the back or a special compliment on a job well done as you run your home and care for yourself. Share kindly language to you from you. Consider calling a friend or family member to see how that person is doing, listening and sharing in your turn.

New Eyes for Family Ties

Family relationships can be terrific and tough at the same time. Many of us experience the land-mine magic of growing up with others, surviving good and tough times together, and still loving one another. For most, ample fodder exists for the grudges and sidekick resentment that can sour relationships and interactions if allowed. None of us is without flaws, and all of us make mistakes. Yet our Lord Jesus says we are to "forgive everyone who is indebted to us" (Luke 11:4); forgive as we are forgiven.

When a conflict reaches the point of impasse or even estrangement, we can pray for fresh eyes and an unbiased heart to understand what happened and why. We can admit we don't always know the details and don't have to know them in order to work through what has happened to us. Sometimes there's large-scale betrayal or trauma or broken trust. We can seek the help of a professional therapist who can listen and help us navigate the hurt and live in the present. We can acknowledge the past and work on new strategies toward a balanced and healthy future. It can be tough but valuable work.

Some of you are in the thick of such conflict now and are praying for reconciliation as you work with a counselor. Feeling the heartbreak but taking steps. God is right there with you, friend. Don't give up! He loves a peacemaker.

Forgiveness is a necessary part of living with others, but it is no easy task. With God's help, we can add this essential skill to our tool belt (we will need it all our lives). On our own power, we can't complete the forgiveness transaction; we just don't have the juice. But we can rely on Him. Through the Holy Spirit, we can ask God to forgive us and release us from the grip of bitterness. We can ask Him to help us forgive others and release them (and us) from the baggage of sin. We can ask others to forgive us, and approach family members in humility and love with the goal of reconciliation. We can accept forgiveness from our heavenly Father and from one another.

Sometimes, though, we remember our painful mistakes and express sorrow and feel shame over and over (and over) again. Or we behave as if we've forgiven a hurt but instead let it fester inside, growing into resentment that spills over into relationships.

Forgiveness is Spirit-led forward thinking. It allows us to move forward, released from the poison we carry when we continue to blame ourselves and others (no matter the fault).

We can power up an ongoing forgiveness process in our families. We regularly mess up, we do or don't do things, and we sometimes offend others with our words and actions. When we hurt others—intentionally or not—we can ask for forgiveness and make it right. Sincere and contrite words such as "I'm sorry," "I blew it," "Please forgive me" can help restore relationships. And if such words don't fix things, we've taken the right step and can release the situation to God in prayer. We can ask for His help in exactly how to restore broken relationships. It's okay to tell others they have hurt us, and be prepared to share forgiveness when requested.

Every family has members who are forgotten, difficult, far away, or live outside the family norms. Perhaps you are the one who is on the outside or is the difficult one (or both!). Whatever the case, let's look anew at those we may have been holding at arm's length or keeping at a distance. By taking one small step at a time, we can begin again to touch these lives, to connect, and to work to build or rebuild relationships with the shine that comes from Jesus. Ask for His help.

The reality? Because of sin and our own imperfections, we hurt those we love. But we have new encouragement that Jesus Himself promises: "Blessed are the peacemakers, for they shall be called sons of God" (Matthew 5:9). From James, the half-brother of Jesus, we also receive this guiding verse:

> But the wisdom from above is first pure, then peaceable, gentle, open to reason, full of mercy and good fruits, impartial and sincere. And a harvest of righteousness is sown in peace by those who make peace. (James 3:17–18)

Jesus wants us to be reconciled with family members, just as we are reconciled to the Father as we confess our sins and receive the forgiveness Jesus won for us on the cross.

The other side of forgiveness and recovering precious family relationships is the good practice of proactively and intentionally fostering positive family interactions. By intentionally pouring time and love into our family relationships on an ongoing basis, we add kindness, interest, and care. Let's pay attention. Let's make time to talk together, to call or visit one another every so often. Let's check in and notice and connect the life-dots. As we say in Spanish, *poco a poco* (little by little), we invest in our relationships.

When we're on the phone or with a family member, let's give that person our full, sweet attention. Can I hear an "amen" for putting away phones at meals and family gatherings?

Such investments in family pay off when something hurtful happens—and it usually does, because we're all sinners. Having a solid foundation built on good times together can help families weather troubles and bolster relationships. As we forgive and are forgiven, the important behaviors of ongoing, positive connecting and investing will sustain and maintain our relationships.

Yet, with some family members, you might be on shaky ground, or you may be building your relationship little by little. Maybe you've got a family member who is bounding through the family boundaries or who has completely shut you out. If you get stuck or feel like you're losing ground, seek help getting unstuck!

Open for Discussion

Our world is politically polarized. We've all noticed growing conflict and disagreement on all fronts. An especially disturbing trend is for folks to cut off family members who have differing viewpoints. A "variety pack" of beliefs can create trouble and take joy out of family gatherings. To be sure, in some situations, it may be important to establish boundaries to protect ourselves from harm or abuse. But generally, let's work to live by more gracious rules of conduct with our own people, our family:

- Leave space in the conversation for all participants and include everyone (even the shy one, the conflict avoider, and the one with whom we often disagree).

- Wait for the other person to finish talking before sharing our thoughts. (Oops!)

- Be curious, ask questions, and be open to hearing what other folks have to say.

- Skip approaching others and entering conversations with a superior or always-right position. (Ouch!)

- Keep civility, grace, and kindness throughout.

- Keep loved ones close and communication open despite differences.

By the way, I'm guilty on all counts for the above. I love to be "right." I need to be better at following this guidance: "Know this, my beloved brothers: let every person be quick to hear, slow to speak, slow to anger" (James 1:19).

The Bible doesn't say: "Lo, if you do not agree with me, so shall I not like or talk with you ever again." Nope. We can peacefully share our views and listen to others, despite differences, creating a continuing dialogue and staying in relationship. Does our sense of rightness, even sometimes competitiveness, need to stand down a bit? What about what Luther says in his explanation of the Eighth Commandment, which encourages us to "explain everything in the kindest way"?

Colossians 3:12–13 also guides us:

> **Put on then, as God's chosen ones, holy and beloved, compassionate hearts, kindness, humility, meekness, and patience, bearing with one another and, if one has a complaint against another, forgiving each other; as the Lord has forgiven you, so you also must forgive.**

Generational conflict, in particular, seems to be at an all-time high. Younger generations have always seen things a little differently than their elders, but the disparity between generations feels wider than ever. Sometimes incongruence occurs because neither (or both) older and younger generations is aware of new or historical information, data, studies, or facts.

As we talk together, let's embrace gentle sharing instead of inflammatory statements. We all have the right to our opinions and free speech. Yes, you be you. But in the process of talking with those around us, let's have respectful conversations and not declare war or start a fire with accusations, stereotypes, or incendiary arguments. Let's ask questions to better understand the perspectives of others and share our beliefs with gentle, considerate words.

Conversation is a team sport. Let's take turns when we're talking together to make sure each person is heard. We can invite others into the discussion with kind, relevant questions. We can give our answer and pass the ball to the next person, asking for his or her thoughts, not dominating but graciously including everyone. (Sometimes I get the "talks" and leave little room for others to share. Help!)

Let's stay receptive and learn. Questions like "What has this looked like to you?" can refresh a dialogue. As we are reminded in Romans 14:19, "So then let us pursue what makes for peace and for mutual upbuilding." Certainly, on some issues, we can embrace the old phrase "Let's agree to disagree." And no, this doesn't mean giving in or failing somehow. We can remain anchored in God's Word and be open to learning and sharing our beliefs. We can hold fast in grace and empathy and continue in conversation. (Perhaps if we model it in our homes, it will spread to our country's leaders?)

My mom has unique perspectives that were shaped as she grew up during World War II. She had relatives who served in the armed forces, some giving their lives. Her early years were filled with the mentality of great national sacrifice to keep our country—and other countries around the world—free from authoritarian empires. My mom values our societal freedom and knows it was won at great cost. When I listen to her stories and the stories of other elders, I learn things about life and get a greater awareness for why things are the way they are today. I learn more about my country and the world. Elders can bring important information and historical depth to our current debates.

Differences in perspective, in generational placement, can add to our family differences. Our United States history is filled with tremendous and tragic times. I love my country, but it's okay to acknowledge the imperfection. The mistakes. The progress or lack of progress in certain matters. Imperfection and beauty are part of our history, just as they live in each of us. And our nation, despite its faults, is still a great country, a place of freedom and opportunity. I celebrate the good and encourage efforts to help and strengthen our citizenry, not divide and destabilize. Where can we work together, uniting perspectives for the common good?

Regarding our younger generations, I wouldn't miss being in relationship with our three adult children for anything. Do we agree on some things? Yep. Do we agree on everything? Nope. Are they smart, engaged, thinking people? Yep. Have they helped me see things in new ways, shared new information, and opened my mind in new ways? Yep. (To be honest, I don't agree with my husband on everything either, but I still love him dearly.) Let's make the effort to stay engaged with people of all ages in our midst and stay informed on the issues. Let's continue to talk and listen and love.

Family relationships can be messy and lovely. Let's keep our minds and hearts open to serve and share the Lord with those around us, including those He has blessed us with as family.

Opportunities to shine the Gospel light appear when we are engaged with others. We can follow God's plan and the Spirit's leading to love with gracious kindness and compassion those who are different from us. Even in disagreement, let's seek to stay connected.

POINTS TO PONDER (INDIVIDUALLY OR IN A SMALL GROUP, BOOK CLUB, OR BIBLE STUDY)

- Can we approach family members with an open heart, engaging with interest and curiosity—even if we disagree on a subject?

- What new thoughts do you have about your family relationships after reading this chapter?

- With whom in our families do we need to prepare the way in prayer to reconcile, connect, forgive, or engage?

ACTION CHALLENGE

- Spend some time journaling about a challenging family relationship this week. Pray for God to help you see or help or talk with this person in a new way.

- Consider adopting one new healthy habit when it comes to interactions with your family.

- This week, what baby step will you take to reconnect or reconcile with a distanced or difficult family member?

PRAYER

Almighty Father, we praise You for Your creation and Your provision here on earth in the form of family. Forgive us for our selfish and hurtful actions to those in our family. Thank You for our loved ones. We need Your love and forgiveness and strength as we navigate the hurts, differences, and challenges between us. May Your Spirit coach us in Your better ways. Show us and lead us to where we can be more flexible and generous. Help us to notice, listen, and better reflect Your light with those in our home and family. May we be an advocate for Your goodness and peace. In the holy name of Jesus. Amen.

CHAPTER 8
ALL AROUND THE NEIGHBORHOOD

BIBLICAL ANCHOR: LUKE 10:27

You shall love the Lord your God with all your heart and with all your soul and with all your strength and with all your mind, and your neighbor as yourself.

KEY TAKEAWAY

With the Holy Spirit working in and through us, we can continue our ministries forward by connecting with those who live and work closest to us—our neighbors. Sometimes we don't know or haven't yet connected with those close by. This is all too common in these busy times. Let's reach out and pursue or continue new, caring interactions with those we encounter in this next circle, even people who may be different from us. One step at a time!

Who Is My Neighbor?

Have you heard about Cornelius? I love his brief mention in the book of Acts, where God included a reference to this leader for us to consider today:

At Caesarea there was a man named Cornelius, a centurion of what was known as the Italian Cohort, a devout man who feared God with all his household, gave alms generously to the people, and prayed continually to God.

> About the ninth hour of the day he saw clearly in a vision an angel of God come in and say to him, "Cornelius." And he stared at him in terror and said, "What is it, Lord?" And he said to him, "Your prayers and your alms have ascended as a memorial before God." (Acts 10:1–4)

God noticed Cornelius's generous, spiritually grounded life, daily prayers, and help for others in need. His life is even more remarkable when we realize that Cornelius was a Roman centurion and was among the class of powerful, wealthy military leaders. He is thought to be one of the first Gentile converts to Christianity. We may not have the sort of position and historical significance that Cornelius had, but God notices our actions too, including our prayers and kindnesses to the folks next door, across the street, and down the block.

In the Houston, Texas, region where I live, we've seen neighbors help neighbors in times of great need. In 2017, during Hurricane Harvey, the south side of our neighborhood was flooded. All around us, the power was out and the roads were flooded, making help from the outside or escape to another area impossible. But in disaster, there can be unexpected loveliness.

Our home was just above the flood line, so I walked to the other side of our neighborhood. Our homeowner's association had set up an area just north of the flooding to gather people and resources. Folks were using small watercraft to rescue neighbors from flooded homes.

Before too long, a kayak came into view, carrying a woman about my age. The Spirit said to me, almost audibly, "This one is for you." I stepped forward to invite this new friend, Michelle, into our home, never having seen or met her before. Michelle agreed to come with me, as her friends weren't able to reach her due to all the flooding. We got a ride back to my home from someone neither of us knew. She was welcomed into our family amidst the chaos.

I resist sharing this story as I don't want to give myself any special credit. You would have done the same. Michelle would have done the same for us. Today, we're her "flood family." She often joins us for holiday meals and is one of our very best friends. She has taught me much about kindness, opportunity, and the importance of advocacy. Truth is, I needed to learn important lessons from Michelle. Thank You, dear God, for connecting us!

Somehow, it's easier to connect with neighbors when there's urgency, like in a natural disaster, but not so much in busy normalcy. It takes interest and persistence, eyes out for folks in silent need right around us. What opportunities do you have to connect in your neighborhood?

Yet it isn't easy to connect in every neighborhood or with every neighbor. When we moved to the area, our neighborhood was fairly new. Everyone seemed more likely to say hello or start a conversation. (Some of the other places we've lived weren't as open.) In the day-to-day, we have a group of neighborhood friends that meets for lunch or coffee regularly and helps one another with small things like gathering the mail when one is on vacation. These relationships have been built through days, weeks, and months of small interactions and gestures.

For example, one time my sunshiny neighbor Janet, who leads us on all kinds of fun adventures, texted me at about 10:00 p.m.: "Are you all done in your garage? Your door is still open." Oops! We hadn't realized it and were grateful for her noticing and letting us know. With new attentiveness, several months later, I was out for a walk and noticed another neighbor's garage door was open but without a car inside. With a quick text, I learned the neighbor was in another part of town and had no idea it was open. I was able to close the door and pay the favor forward.

Another neighbor, Susan, lives in quiet kindness to others and is a paper artist. She makes beautiful handmade cards and other cool creations. At our church, we love to have everyone sign and send cards to folks to say thank you, get well, or that they are in our prayers. I asked Susan if she would be willing to make cards for our church to send out. We were glad to pay for her artistry, but Susan insisted on creating a generous supply for us to use as her gift to our church. We are grateful. Many hearts have been blessed by receiving a gorgeous, handmade card signed by dozens of fellow members.

My neighbor Mercedes is a bright and brave spirit. Whether she's helping others or up in a hot-air balloon, she's both caring and adventurous. I want to be more like her. (Mercedes also has a secret weapon: her dog, Maggie, is the dearest doggie and brings joy to all. When I have the chance to greet and pet her, I receive a jolt of happiness.)

And there's our can-do neighbor, Bunny, who truly can do anything. (I've even seen her use a chainsaw.) She's a part-time volunteer at a thrift shop that benefits people in need in our communities. At other times, Bunny travels to disaster areas as part of a relief team. Between times, she's a grandma, helping out her kids by caring for her grandkids.

These precious friendships were developed with action and attention, grace and forgiveness, mingled with a bit of fun and laughter. Still, there are neighbors right beside me where some smaller, intentional acts of kindness could start or continue to build relationships. I, too, have work to do. Guide me, Lord!

In our everyday situations, large and small, we can connect with and help others in meaningful ways. God works through His people in times of disaster and in ordinary daily life.

Stepping Out

With our modern home architecture, many of us miss even seeing our neighbors as we drive into automatic-door-opening garages and walk right into our homes, never stepping outside. Others live in small towns and rural settings, where houses are farther apart and neighbors are more distant. Maybe you're in an apartment and your neighbors are very close indeed.

Perhaps you've already connected to your neighbors, and you help one another out and have one another's back. Cool. While my husband and I have developed rich friendships with many of our neighbors, there are close-by neighbors that we don't know. It's been gnawing on me to better connect to those who live right around us. The Bible encourages us in our neighboring:

> Let each of us please his neighbor for his good, to build him up. (Romans 15:2)

> For the whole law is fulfilled in one word: "You shall love your neighbor as yourself." (Galatians 5:14)

Other verses focus on what *not* to do: we should not give false witness against our neighbor (Exodus 20:16) or plot evil against our neighbor (Zechariah 8:17). Contrasting with these, God's Word tells us to seek the good of our neighbor (1 Corinthians 10:24). God shows us in multiple instances throughout His Word that our neighbor relationships are important and in these important relationships we can show the love of Christ.

We are also reminded in the Ten Commandments that we aren't to covet or steal anything that belongs to our neighbors. As my husband says, adding a Texas interpretation, "Not even their brand-new, fully loaded truck."

God is interested in our neighborliness. In the Bible, He's given us good directions and advice, with instructions for what to do and what not to do. Wherever we dwell, small steps are good steps. We can start or keep going from where we are now, building and maintaining good relationships with our neighbors.

Connect to Care

What makes a good neighbor? Reflecting on our neighboring over the years, I would suggest that kind interaction and timely assistance when needed are two great acts. What do you think?

I was on the phone with my friend and colleague Laura Pulliam when she gave a quick apology and abruptly ended the call. Her next-door neighbor, frantic with alarm, had reached out for help—their barbeque grill was on fire! Laura quickly grabbed her fire extinguisher, put the fire out, and called me back. Amazing. She was there, kindly and availably, to help when needed.

Not all help is this timely and dramatic, so what might be a first step? Friendly greetings and starting a conversation when we see our neighbors are always good. We can offer to gather our neighbors' mail and water the plants during vacations. We can share baked goods at holiday times or host a friendly neighborhood barbeque or ice cream social to introduce and connect folks. We can take a moment to chat, to ask how they're doing, to learn more about them, and to show genuine interest.

When my husband and I were first married, we lived next door to an elderly couple. How many hours we spent with those two! They had time to listen, time to care. We could go on and on about work or life or whatever, and they were always there for us in kindness, patience, and wisdom. What a blessing!

Let's survey our neighbors today. Let's take a tiny step with the neighbors we don't know. That said, sometimes neighboring can be tough. There are some neighbors we don't often see or who don't return our greeting. If we have a troubled relationship with a neighbor, we can pray for reconciliation and peace, looking for ways to move the relationship in a positive direction. Even if it looks like the way is closed and there is little hope (I've been there), keep taking baby steps as you are able. Let's not be *that* neighbor (read on).

I love to grow hyacinth beans. They have a lovely purple vine and a sweet pea–like blossom. Several years ago, I planted seeds on the side of our house near the fence we shared with the neighbor. The vines grew and thrived, climbing on and falling over onto our neighbor's side. I told myself, *Oh, it's so pretty, they won't mind.* Our neighbors didn't say anything, but I wasn't being fair with my neighbor: my plant was on their side of the fence. The next year, I had a talk with myself, and now the plants are on our side of the fence only. A tidy hibiscus blooms where our fence meets theirs. No encroachment.

Viva la Difference!

Neighbors (and we) can be a blessing, an inconvenience, and sometimes even a trial. As we have seen from Scripture, neighborliness is on God's mind. Sometimes we're in great need of His help with our neighbors. And while it's more convenient to live as we are now, with the relationships as they are, let's resolve to move forward as we are able. Author Shannan Martin encourages us:

> Mutual trust and easy affection won't erase the ills of our wonky, wobbly world. We've got buckets of work to do, but beginning with a clear sense of solidarity is a great place to begin. Making one neighborhood more connected makes the world more connected. The math checks out. Here's to inching away from the familiar. Here's to trusting ourselves and each other more every day.[24]

A micro approach to building a larger sense of community makes sense. When we work to connect, to get along with our neighbors, we are also positively impacting the greater community and world. We don't need to be afraid to engage if our neighbors are different from us. When we close our hearts to our neighbors who are different, we miss opportunities to engage and share the light of Jesus. When we "wear" Christ, we draw others to Him. Let's stay solid in our faith without communicating superiority or self-righteousness to others. I love the way the apostle Paul talks about living our faith: "You yourselves are our letter of recommendation, written on our hearts, to be known and read by all" (2 Corinthians 3:2).

As Christians, our lives are precious, imperfect stories that tell of how we have been redeemed by Christ; we can tell that story to all we encounter. For the Gospel to spread, our encountering must go beyond our friends and fellow church members. When we spend time only with other believers and folks who "think like us," we are missing the mission field!

---

24 Shannan Martin, *Start with Hello: And Other Simple Ways to Live as Neighbors* (Grand Rapids, MI: Revell, 2022), 52–53.

I love this encouraging description from Revelation:

After this I looked, and behold, a great multitude that no one could number, from every nation, from all tribes and peoples and languages, standing before the throne and before the Lamb, clothed in white robes, with palm branches in their hands, and crying out with a loud voice, "Salvation belongs to our God who sits on the throne, and to the Lamb!" And all the angels were standing around the throne and around the elders and the four living creatures, and they fell on their faces before the throne and worshiped God, saying, "Amen! Blessing and glory and wisdom and thanksgiving and honor and power and might be to our God forever and ever! Amen." (Revelation 7:9–12)

In addition to our families, let's step forward to more or new neighbors, to people who may be different from us. Gently. With grace. On our walks. As we shop, work, or garden. As we travel our days. Kingdom moments come from the Holy Spirit as we become vessels for His purpose everywhere we go.

Yes, I'm working on this, and so can you. Let's connect and share the light of Christ that is in us but not from us. By the work of the Holy Spirit, we can offer ourselves for God's use and put competitiveness and exclusivity to the side. In our neighborhoods, with the people nearby, let's open our hearts to the Spirit's leading to share Christ's message, living and breathing in us!

POINTS TO PONDER (INDIVIDUALLY OR IN A SMALL GROUP, BOOK CLUB, OR BIBLE STUDY)

- Where do you have good neighborly relationships? Not so good?

- Envision some first steps to connect with neighbors you don't yet know; what are those steps?

- Think about your relationships with your neighbors; how can those relationships be improved?

ACTION CHALLENGE

- Pray for your neighbors specifically this week.

- Take a first step to build a positive relationship with one of your neighbors.

- Keep your eyes open for ways you can help, serve, and connect with your neighbors.

- Consider hosting some kind of neighborly get-together, Bible study, or other social gathering to connect with those nearby in a new, neighborly way.

PRAYER

Gracious Father, You created the universe, and You also created our neighbors. You have placed us where we are for Your purposes. Forgive our sometimes-insular life that skips connection with those living nearby. By Your Spirit, help us to really see our neighbors, to connect and serve as we are able. Where barriers exist, by Your power make a way for us to restore and build positive relationships, step by step. May the light You provide lead the way in our day-to-day neighborliness. In Your dear Son Jesus' name. Amen.

CHAPTER 9
EVERYWHERE I GO

BIBLICAL ANCHOR: MATTHEW 5:14-16

You are the light of the world. A city set on a hill cannot be hidden. Nor do people light a lamp and put it under a basket, but on a stand, and it gives light to all in the house. In the same way, let your light shine before others, so that they may see your good works and give glory to your Father who is in heaven.

KEY TAKEAWAY

God shows us people with whom we can share His light and love in our neighborhoods, and as we go about our day with errands, travels, classes, appointments, workplaces, and other journey spaces. Lord, let us see others with Your eyes in our every day. Wherever we go and whoever we encounter in our daily lives, may our hearts be open for Your purposes!

Mobile Shine

This is fun! God provides opportunities for us to shine and serve wherever we go. We can share our faith with our postal carriers, trash pickup people, grocery store clerks, medical staff, clients, coworkers, acquaintances, family at home, and extended family. Around the house and out and about. Whoever we meet, wherever we go. Today and every day.

Places and spaces for divine appointments are often ordinary. Recently, my husband scheduled a medical treatment. We were there early in the day, and the process took a few hours. As time passed, the waiting area began to fill up with other folks and we began to chat. Then, as we prepared to leave, Raymond asked the lady nearest to us, "Would you like me to pray for you?" She nodded. He looked around. Other heads nearby also joined in and nodded. He went on to say a beautiful prayer of trust, strength, healing, and hope despite medical difficulties. Despite our troubles, despite their troubles, we were all lifted by the power of prayer. I felt a connection and a shift in the place.

In today's impersonal culture, our outreach is more important than ever. When we share a "mobile shine," we combat the lack of civility that seems to be everywhere. Recently, my husband, my mom, and I were traveling and had just arrived at the airport. My mom needs to use elevators instead of stairs. We waited in line with other families, with elderly people and babies in strollers. When it was our turn, a fully capable couple simply walked faster and cut in line ahead of us, taking our place in the elevator. Yes, they knew what they were doing. They "got there first."

Selfish behavior is easy to fall into when we are inconvenienced, when we don't get our way or don't get to be first or have to wait. It happens on the highway, at restaurants, and in checkout lines—in our day-to-day spaces.

Once when I was at the grocery store, the man ahead of me in line began to get angry at the cashier. His purchase was more expensive than he expected. The cashier tried to find a coupon that would help defray the cost, but to no avail. Finally, in frustration, the man said, "I'm going to talk to your manager." After my purchase was complete, I waited, standing quietly until the man finished his complaint. Then, after he left, I approached the manager and offered another perspective on what had happened. The next time I shopped, the cashier was still working there, thanks be to God. The man may have been upset about rising food prices—it *is* upsetting—but it didn't make sense to take it out on those who aren't at fault, people who are working hard and who didn't cause the price increase.

Let's try again. In mercy. In grace. In humility. In kindness. For years, I didn't know our postal carrier's name. Now I do, and I love the friendship I have with this lovely woman. I say "thank you" for her daily service to us and our community, and sometimes I offer her a cold drink on a hot day or leave a little treat or note in the mailbox for her. Yes, she is simply doing her job, but what an essential one! Getting to know her has brought me joy.

When we determine to try again, we need a place to start. Perhaps that can be putting a couple of those delicious cookies you just baked (or bought) in your mailbox. At Christmas, my mom likes to share a jar of homemade jam, lovingly made by one of the ladies from her mission group, with all kinds of folks as her expression of appreciation in a world that seems to have forgotten kindness.

Our garbage collectors are so fast that they're hard to catch. But every so often, especially when it's really hot, we are able to run out in time to share cold sports drinks along with a quick wave and thank you. Is it a small act? Yes. Is it shining? I think so. I like looking for opportunities God places before me to shine His light. No, I don't do it perfectly, and neither will you. But we can do the best we can with what we have: we can let someone go ahead of us, give away things we no longer need, put in a good word for someone at work or in the neighborhood, smile at people—the list goes on and on because the love of Jesus goes on and on. As we show kindness to people, the door may open for us to share the reason: because we have experienced the light of forgiveness that Christ shone on us in His death and resurrection, we can't help but shine it on others.

One of the easiest things we can do is "see" the people who help us—or whom we help—as divinely created, unique, and precious human beings and say to them, "God bless you!"

We often have opportunities to thank people with respect for the help they've given or to return the received help with kindness. When we're the ones helping, we can show God's grace as we serve. As author and mental health care provider Heidi Goehmann encourages us, wherever we are:

> In the quiet, in the wrestling and writing, and in the glamour, this is what I have discovered: we simply are asked to enter in. Mindfully aware of our limits, we enter into the life God has called us to by putting us in this time and space. We are created to connect in whatever spaces we've been given. I will enter into mine with my whole heart. May you enter into yours, friends. May you enter into yours.[25]

Jesus Leads the Way

Jesus shows us, over and over again, a way to approach ministry His way. That includes being open to others, no matter who they are. The same or different. He accepted people as individuals, all imperfect (like us) and worthy of His notice.

---

25 Heidi Goehmann (@lifeinrelationshippodcast), Instagram post. August 2, 2022.

He avoided and even chastised the Pharisees and other leaders who, in self-created superiority, held themselves above others, pretending to know it all and be without sin, showing no mercy (Matthew 9:11–13).

The Savior of the world leaned in then, and He leans in now. Amazing, isn't it, how He interacts in loving awareness of all the details, choosing to meet people right where they are, with no scolding or shaming. He graciously includes each one of us, as lowly as we are, in His plan of salvation and Gospel mission—an upside-down way of leading a revolution, with ordinary people like us as main characters.

We can graciously serve those around us in Jesus' name. Without criticism. Without self-righteousness. Without condemnation. We can open our arms and hearts with a loving and alert approach. We can ask respectful questions. We can be willing to be inconvenienced. Let's help others as they wish or need to be helped, without doing for them that which they can do for themselves.

Time, attention, and care, for the rich and the poor, for those who have it all and for those who are struggling. Isolation and loneliness create a need for connection and conversation. The elderly. New moms. Us. Our pent-up words and feelings can yearn for a trusted, patient, and listening ear. Text or call that relative or old friend, and take time to talk, ask questions, and listen; to take a step forward in the relationship. Acknowledge the need to share and listen in turn.

Recently, I arrived at the pharmacy and there was no line. (Yes!) I began a conversation with the employee helping me, starting with legitimate questions but drifting into chat. To my dismay, when I finally released this gracious soul from my need to talk, five people were waiting in line behind me. We are created for community and relationship, which means that most of us need to talk with someone and be heard. In this instance, rather than inconveniencing the people in line behind me, perhaps I would have been better off seeking out a friend or family member to share and listen.

Shining the light starts with Christ, with the compassion He shows us by coming near to us in His Word, by seeking us when we stray, and by forgiving our sin. When we know His abundant love, we can turn to others with kindness and service.

There's a larger store where I shop monthly. Over time, I've gotten to know an employee there, a cashier. Our conversation began with my mom's "snack ministry." When checking out at the store, I asked this cashier if he'd like a snack or drink for his break. The answer? "Yes, a share size bag of M&Ms, please." He looked forward to sharing the treat with his granddaughter when she got home from school. After a couple of visits and bags of M&Ms, he told me his granddaughter had just achieved the honor roll at her school after a great deal of hard work and persistence. He asked, "Would you mind writing her a little note of encouragement?" I was happy to do as he asked, writing my words of affirmation on receipt paper. We've continued to talk (briefly, of course, respecting his job), and he knows that he and his family are in my daily prayers.

Serve with What You've Got

As a kid, I loved to read a book called *Eight Bags of Gold*.[26] It's a bright retelling of Jesus' parable of the talents, written for children. In biblical days, a talent was a monetary unit of

---

26 Janice Kramer, *Eight Bags of Gold: Matthew 25:14–30 for Children* (St. Louis: Concordia Publishing House, 1964).

sizable value. A silver talent was worth more than twenty years' wages, a gold talent thirty times more. Big stuff. Let's review the biblical text:

> For it will be like a man going on a journey, who called his servants and entrusted to them his property. To one he gave five talents, to another two, to another one, to each according to his ability. Then he went away. He who had received the five talents went at once and traded with them, and he made five talents more. So also he who had the two talents made two talents more. But he who had received the one talent went and dug in the ground and hid his master's money. Now after a long time the master of those servants came and settled accounts with them. And he who had received the five talents came forward, bringing five talents more, saying, "Master, you delivered to me five talents; here, I have made five talents more." His master said to him, "Well done, good and faithful servant. You have been faithful over a little; I will set you over much. Enter into the joy of your master." And he also who had the two talents came forward, saying, "Master, you delivered to me two talents; here, I have made two talents more." His master said to him, "Well done, good and faithful servant. You have been faithful over a little; I will set you over much. Enter into the joy of your master." He also who had received the one talent came forward, saying, "Master, I knew you to be a hard man, reaping where you did not sow, and gathering where you scattered no seed, so I was afraid, and I went and hid your talent in the ground. Here, you have what is yours." But his

master answered him, "You wicked and slothful servant! You knew that I reap where I have not sown and gather where I scattered no seed? Then you ought to have invested my money with the bankers, and at my coming I should have received what was my own with interest. So take the talent from him and give it to him who has the ten talents. For to everyone who has will more be given, and he will have an abundance. But from the one who has not, even what he has will be taken away. And cast the worthless servant into the outer darkness. In that place there will be weeping and gnashing of teeth." (Matthew 25:14–30)

As with all of Jesus' parables, these verses share an earthly story with a heavenly meaning. When I read these passages today, in the context of our conversation together, here's what stands out:

- Even only one talent is highly valuable.

- We are called to make the best use we can with whatever talent or talents God has given us.

- Even if we have only one talent, it is of great worth, and we can honor God with it. We can enter into service with joy, giving the glory to God.

I am in the one-talent category. I am not a good cook, can't play the piano or fix things, sometimes struggle with technology, and am best as a "backup" singer. In ministry life, my husband and I serve at a small mission church. It was launched in 1937 to serve Spanish-speaking people in downtown Houston. Even after nearly a century of existence, it is still not big or influential. And yet, God is doing wonderful things there. He brought my husband to serve as pastor for the precious people of this congregation, in this place, for His kingdom. Big numbers aren't the definition of important. Our church is important. We have beautiful people and purpose even in our small space. You, too, are important in the Lord's eyes and for His loving purposes.

God, in His mysterious and all-knowing ways, loves and cares about us and the people around us. He places us in our locations and vocations for His purposes. Each and every person in our tiny congregation is important to Him. So are you!

If you have mobility challenges, take heart. Your prayers, phone conversations, and interactions with those around you can be powerful for the Lord. At our last church, we had a good friend who got around on a scooter and had other health issues. And yet, she often called folks (even me!) to check in and see how they were doing. She lifted many people with her sweet interest and prayer support.

God sees everything and knows everything. He provides opportunities for us, powered by the Spirit. When we embrace our humility and open ourselves to His service, God can use our lives in very powerful ways for the Kingdom. Big ways and little ways. One talent, two talents, or five talents. All are valuable. Maybe you're in a small place or space too. Your purpose there is still important. Don't bury your talent, my friend!

When God Orchestrates the Circumstances

We know that God works in the small things for extraordinary purposes. Sometimes these small acts are part of a bigger picture. Let me share a story.

We've employed a landscaping crew for eight years now. They do a great job of making our yard look terrific. We welcome their work with a warm hello, a cold sports drink (Houston, right?), and a granola bar.

One of the workers, José, is a gregarious fellow. He always has a smile and a friendly greeting for us, even though he's hard at work and sweating it out in our hot and humid climate. About a year ago, my mom noticed that he hadn't worked with the crew for several weeks. We checked in with the company owner and learned that José was having medical issues. We kept an eye out for his return, and when he came back, we asked if he needed anything. As we talked together, it was obvious that he was having difficulties and we could see other evidence of his illness. We asked José if we could take him to the doctor or the hospital. His employer had already offered, but José had refused, even though he is a longtime employee, almost like family. And at first, José said no to us too. His past included deeply negative experiences with hospitals and doctors.

But the severity of his symptoms continued, and the next week, we asked again. This time, José accepted our offer and plans were made for the trip. His availability coincided with my jury duty summons, but my husband, Raymond, was happy to take him. As they headed off to the hospital, José still wasn't feeling well, and just as they arrived at the emergency room entrance, he got very ill indeed. When Raymond stopped the car, José opened the car door and fell out of the car and collapsed onto the pavement. The ER's response was swift. A half dozen workers ran out to lift him onto a stretcher and take him inside for immediate attention. The diagnosis: a stroke.

Later, the ER doctor asked Raymond exactly what time they arrived at the hospital. The kind of stroke José experienced had a small window when medication could prevent most of the negative impact of the event. The doctor had been able to give José the medication he needed just in time to prevent disability or even death.

When we visited him in the hospital the next day, José was unconscious. The room was full of beeping machines, monitoring his vitals and keeping him alive. Raymond commended him to the Lord's eternal care, and we prayed over him. Over the next few days, José's condition improved dramatically. The medication had been administered in time to prevent the worst. He was going to be okay!

Now when José works at our house, I always greet him with a hug; he is dear to us. And José knows—he absolutely knows—that God loves him and watches out for him. He knows the Holy Spirit made a special effort to connect us with him exactly when he needed urgent medical attention. He knows God opened up time and availability for my husband to take him to the hospital. José knows he is important to God because the Spirit inspired a way for those around him to quite possibly save his life. Not because José has high status or is an influencer. But because he is a beloved, valued child of God. Like you. Like me. I've taken José to a couple of medical appointments since then; he knows we're here for him.

Although helping others can be inconvenient, we can be sure that God has us where we can best serve others. A small act can be big indeed. Shining the light of Jesus most often starts small and often remains small. It's more like a slow cooker than a microwave. I love the way author and leader Rev. Dr. John Arthur Nunes describes this kind of "slow work":

Slow work isn't working slowly. Rather, it means to pace yourself, at least for a preplanned slice of life, with a panoramic reflectiveness. Slow work is circumspect, looking around, paying attention to these people with whom you are blessed, seeing the threads of the divine being woven through the seemingly scattershot arc of our all-too-common, often-too-boring, but certainly all-too-complicated lives.[27]

Our heavenly Father gives us the privilege to serve His heavenly purposes: slowly and with the Holy Spirit's divine direction. We can serve quietly, without bringing attention to ourselves. We can serve humbly, surrendering to divine aims. What a gift to be powered up with the goodness of Christ to shine and serve others in His name!

POINTS TO PONDER (INDIVIDUALLY OR IN A SMALL GROUP, BOOK CLUB, OR BIBLE STUDY)

- What are ways your time and talents serve God and others in your daily life?

- However many talents God has blessed you with, how can you expand your spiritual care to others in your every day, guided and powered by the Holy Spirit?

- Consider the concept of "slow work." How do you think this kind of work is different from typical life in our fast-paced society?

---

27 John Arthur Nunes, *Meant for More: In, With, and Under the Ordinary* (St. Louis: Concordia Publishing House, 2020), 156.

ACTION CHALLENGE

- Make a mental list of your talents, special experiences, affiliations, and location.

- Serve someone with your talents this week, even if it's "only" with the golden but underappreciated trio of caring: your time, attention, and listening ear.

- Look for ways to slow down this week, to set aside distractions to simply be there for someone or let someone be there for you.

PRAYER

Almighty Father, we praise You for Your mighty works, for Your goodness and mercy, and for sending Your Son, Jesus, to save us. As we live our daily lives, we love to pursue our own aims. Forgive us for missing Your important work in the details of daily life. Help us to see those around us as individuals, as Your beautiful creations. Remind us that You value every person, and therefore, we can value them as well. May we extend the essence of human equality and mutual caring, civility and grace, dignity and mercy as we interact with others with our whole hearts. Lead us through Your Holy Spirit to shine the light of Christ, that in faith, with kindness and love, we may extend to others the hope and joy and peace that You offer to all. In the name of Your Son, Jesus. Amen.

CHAPTER 10
GOD'S PURPOSE IN YOUR EVERY DAY

BIBLICAL ANCHOR: PROVERBS 11:25

Whoever brings blessing will be enriched, and one who waters will himself be watered.

KEY TAKEAWAY

Although we aren't important or famous, our suffering world needs us, both you and me. God provides situations for us to help and serve others right where we are, right now. The Holy Spirit powers, strengthens, and guides us. The Word and Sacraments sustain us in the Savior. Through His love, one step at a time, our small help adds up to a big impact. As we lean into our faith and lean out in our daily lives, we can share the shine that is from the Lord; it draws people to Him. We can provide hope and encouragement, which in turn gives us purpose and lift, gifts of God's extraordinary grace.

You Are a Gift to the World

The world needs you, and the world needs me. Regardless of how big or small our life is, even if it looks to us that we don't have a big role to play, we can be assured that there's hope that comes from knowing the Lord, knowing He created us, knowing He loves us and has specific purposes for us.

God pays attention to things the world doesn't notice. He has the power, authority, creativity, and will to create the world and everything in it. Although it's hard to comprehend, He individually created you and me. We are the apple of His eye, so of course, He pays attention to us! (See Psalm 17:8; Zechariah 2:8.)

Stay connected to His love for you. Read the Word and be shaped and guided by it. Worship in spirit and truth, receiving the Gospel and the renewal and refreshment of the Lord's Supper. Be filled with the living water Jesus provides. Pray with the confident knowledge that God hears you and cares for you! Thank God for all He has done for you, and serve Him earnestly with your brothers and sisters. Look inside your congregation and outside to your community, where small and thoughtful acts can provide mercy and help.

With new awareness, we serve others in this way and can discover or rediscover purpose. We can celebrate how God uses our lives to impact others. Be encouraged, my friends:

Trust in the LORD, and do good; dwell in the land and befriend faithfulness. Delight yourself in the LORD, and He will give you the desires of your heart. Commit your way to the LORD; trust in Him, and He will act. He will bring forth your righteousness as the light, and your justice as the noonday. (Psalm 37:3-6)

The Bible promises spiritual blessings as we serve:

Whoever pursues righteousness and kindness will find life, righteousness, and honor. (Proverbs 21:21)

We know that God works through people. He extends His power and strength to us through the power of the Holy Spirit. We have things to do: wherever we are, in our own space and place, God has divine purposes for us. Small things are big things. Hope and wait expectantly:

> Do not neglect to do good and to share what you have, for such sacrifices are pleasing to God. (Hebrews 13:16)

What's next? Do you think you're not ready to step forward? Not up to it? Not good enough (or Christian enough or bold enough or smart enough)? No—you're just right. Remember, God created you and loves you (yes, *you*) unconditionally. He leads the way and provides the power. He protects you and forgives you. You will be following His agenda, not yours. You can trust Him completely.

It's okay if you don't have your own reality TV show or social media following or megachurch. You, just as you are, are important to the world and important to God. In humility, you can serve His good purposes right where you are, following this beautiful guidance from the apostle Paul:

> Let love be genuine. Abhor what is evil; hold fast to what is good. Love one another with brotherly affection. Outdo one another in showing honor. Do not be slothful in zeal, be fervent in spirit, serve the Lord. Rejoice in hope, be patient in tribulation, be constant in prayer. Contribute to the needs of the saints and seek to show hospitality.
>
> Bless those who persecute you; bless and do not curse them. Rejoice with those who rejoice, weep with those who weep. Live in harmony with one another. Do not be haughty, but associate with the lowly. Never be wise in your own sight. Repay no one evil for evil, but give

thought to do what is honorable in the sight of all. If possible, so far as it depends on you, live peaceably with all. Beloved, never avenge yourselves, but leave it to the wrath of God, for it is written, "Vengeance is Mine, I will repay, says the Lord." To the contrary, "if your enemy is hungry, feed him; if he is thirsty, give him something to drink; for by so doing you will heap burning coals on his head." Do not be overcome by evil, but overcome evil with good. (Romans 12:9–21)

Purpose Is All around You

Incremental, small steps of kindness make a difference in the lives of others. Little things. Quiet, purposeful deeds shared with respect and compassion. Humble, helpful actions that don't bring attention to ourselves but instead show mercy and point to God for His glory.

The kindness we show in our households and to our families has the purpose of shining the Gospel on those dearest to us. The little things we do at home, at church, at work, where we do business, and where we volunteer have an impact, "for the LORD your God has blessed you in all the work of your hands" (Deuteronomy 2:7). Our efforts, in and through our vocations, and inspired and directed by God through the Holy Spirit, share and show the love that Jesus first showed us.

As we move around in our neighborhoods and communities, may we do so with sensitivity and wisdom, as we look with fresh eyes for the little but vital missions God puts in front of us to encourage and lift others. Let's share His shine with others, to encourage and bless each person we meet. Be strengthened by the Aaronic blessing and the light of Christ:

> The LORD bless you and keep you;
>
> the LORD make His face to shine upon you and be gracious to you;
>
> the LORD lift up His countenance upon you and give you peace. (Numbers 6:24–26)

Embrace the blessing. Embrace His peace. When the Lord shines upon us, we experience His divine love. We are empowered to step out to serve. Helping others gives glory to God and benefits our hurting world. Our kindness to others close by and as we travel about our daily lives is a beautiful reflection of the shining light of Christ.

Let's delight in lovely things: A kindly word. A helpful act. Outreach to the forgotten. Attention to the lonely. Slow things, delivered with time and care.

Ordinary Lives

I'm not holding myself up as someone who has it all figured out. I struggle with relationships and serving, moving forward one step, moving back two. I'm an unlikely helper, preferring to hang out with my sweet husband and mom and read good books, content to sit on the sidelines.

With God's help and leading, I'm slowly and reluctantly engaging in the journey He has opened up—okay, pulled me into. I stumble or succeed and try again.

God has inspired me to shine His light in imperfection and joy. He cares about people; He cares about you; He cares about me. I'm still learning and growing in this work. Join me. Let's encourage one another. I'd love for you to keep in touch and let me know how you are doing, one step at a time.

I'm a one-talent person and an introvert, an ordinary life in a small place. Many people in our city of Houston haven't heard of our congregation. Our church building isn't on "the other side of the tracks"; we are one house away from the railroad tracks.

Raymond and I aren't in the Who's Who of clergy couples. God called my husband into ministry and brought us to this church to serve Him and to tend His flock. Because God is in the detail business, a small church has big importance. God is looking out for all of His children. The work we do where we are now, and wherever we may serve in the future, is valuable because He has placed us there for His purposes.

I'm remembering my great-grandfather, Rev. Jacob Rubel, who graduated from the seminary in 1884 and set out for Minnesota in a covered wagon. (Love this!) He started churches in the farmlands, later moving to Milwaukee to serve a small congregation of German immigrants.

My other great-grandfather, Rev. J. Henry Stoeppelwerth, pioneered west to Kansas to help start a seminary. My grandfather, Rev. W. W. Stoeppelwerth, served as pastor at a university and in towns across the Kansas plains. My father, Rev. Henry Stoeppelwerth, began ministry at a church plant in California and proudly served his country as a chaplain in the US Air Force. He was a deep thinker and innovator, pioneering small groups in the 1970s and thoughtfully leading other congregations in Colorado, Maryland, and Virginia.

These pastors were joined by their wives: my mother, grandmother, and great-grandmothers, who served as ministry partners in spreading the Gospel and were leaders in their own right, loving and Christ-led.

I celebrate this spiritual legacy. And you, reader, for all the souls who came before you to serve the Lord, stand on their shoulders. We benefit from their combined faithfulness, service, and leadership. If you're a new believer or the first in your family to be a believer, welcome. You are beginning your own spiritual legacy. Our histories blend beautifully with one another. All of us were grafted in and are now serving the Lord where He has us: in our families, congregations, neighborhoods, and communities.

We remember the lives of those we love; we remember the graces, the kindnesses. The troubles and faithful perseverance. The small and big acts of courage. All combine to tell a story of wobbly but joy-filled journeys. Sinners and saints. In all things, we celebrate serving the One who created the world and made you and me. Small details of great importance and impact.

With the help of God, and because we are His unique creations, we have our very own work to do. Yahoo!

Extraordinary Grace

As our work continues for the Lord, let's receive fresh encouragement from poet Tanner Olson:

Let all of this be for Your glory, Your good.

Give joy to these feet as they step into the unknown.

Give trust to these hands as they serve with love.

Give grace to my words as they echo the good news
of hope.[28]

Beautiful. I'm a nobody in the world, but with God's help
and leading, I'm a somebody with something to do. Today.
Tomorrow. Always. And so are you!

This is for God's glory, not ours. We are serving in His power
for His purposes. We are always in process: learning, growing,
failing, and returning to the source of the shine—Jesus.

**And we all, with unveiled face, beholding the glory of the
Lord, are being transformed into the same image from
one degree of glory to another. For this comes from the
Lord who is the Spirit. (2 Corinthians 3:18)**

Whoever and wherever you are, Jesus is with you and is
shining through you. One talent, two talents, or five talents.
Ordinary is extraordinary. We step forward together, in quietness and humility, with kindness and compassion. Slowly and
with awareness. With both words and actions, not to save the
world—Christ took care of this already—but to bless someone close to us in His precious name, to connect each soul to
His saving grace.

As we benefit others, God, in His miraculous way, has
planned to benefit us. Receive these wise words from Dr. Steve
Siegle, health professional:

Kindness has been shown to increase self-esteem,
empathy and compassion, and improve mood. It can
decrease blood pressure and cortisol, a hormone directly

---

28 Tanner Olson, "Trust and Surrender," in *Continue: Poems and Prayers of
Hope* (St. Louis: Concordia Publishing House, 2022), 62.

correlated with stress levels. People who give of themselves in a balanced way also tend to be healthier and live longer.

Kindness can increase your sense of connectivity with others, decrease loneliness, combat low mood and improve relationships. It also can be contagious, encouraging others to join in with their own generous deeds.[29]

Don't you just love how God created us to spiritually, physically, and emotionally benefit from serving others? In this way, I believe He is lifting us as we help His children, whoever and wherever they are. Let the Spirit flow through you and empower you for life. Siegle adds this encouragement: "Rather than viewing it exclusively as an action, think of kindness as a quality of being you can cultivate. Giving kindness often is simple, free and health-enhancing."[30] Amen! Lord, lead the way!

Many people in our families, in our neighborhoods, and those we come into contact with in our day-to-day routines lack connection. They may feel hopeless. Many don't know about the grace-filled love of Jesus and His beautiful light. When we approach our ministry from an open, Spirit-led place, we are better able to see, serve, shine, and make a difference in the forever lives of others.

Let's continue forward—small steps by small steps—living out our lives of sanctification, growing in spiritual depth and becoming what God intends for us. As we anchor ourselves in the Lord, may each of us be filled daily with the power and

29 Steve Siegle, "The Art of Kindness" Mayo Clinic Health System, August 17, 2023, https://www.mayoclinichealthsystem.org/hometown-health/speaking-of-health/the-art-of-kindness (accessed November 9, 2023).
30 Siegle, "The Art of Kindness."

direction of the Spirit. May we move as He wills. May our Kingdom-building be filled with mission moments as we convey the love of Christ in our daily spaces.

Walk with me. Discover with me. Offer your every day life to the Lord in a new or bigger way. Shine with me and find purpose and life. My prayer is for God to use this book powerfully in my life and yours!

With whatever time and resources we have, let's shine together! Let us delight and discover God's good purpose in our every day, our ordinary lives transformed by His extraordinary grace!

To Him be the glory!

POINTS TO PONDER (INDIVIDUALLY OR IN A SMALL GROUP, BOOK CLUB, OR BIBLE STUDY)

- What's your spiritual history? How can you celebrate how you and your family shine the light of Christ? If you're new to the faith, how does it feel to start a legacy of faith in your family tree?

- What do you think of ordinary/extraordinary purpose? How do you think the Lord will lead you to shine today and in the days to come?

- How will you welcome God's purpose and lift for your every day? How will you be lifted as you help others, fed and led by the Holy Spirit?

ACTION CHALLENGE

- Take a moment to thank God for your family's spiritual history. Reflect upon the gift of your own faith. If you're the first believer in your family, go you! Write your story, briefly or at length. How has God prepared you to serve Him? Make a collage, write a story, or draw a picture. Celebrate the unique placement God has given you in the world!

- Spend time in devotion to God, to fill you spiritually. Ask Him to lead you to an ordinary/extraordinary way to serve this week. Keep your eyes open in hopeful anticipation for opportunities to serve. Remember, it's small things, one step at a time!

- Celebrate the lift that comes from being open to the inspiration and guidance of the Holy Spirit through you. Give God the glory and enjoy the delight that serving Him brings as you travel your day-to-day journeys. Amen!

PRAYER

Gracious Father, in You, all things were made. In You is no darkness at all. You sent Your beloved Son, Jesus, to save us. We often miss Your purposes, the important, small, and slow actions in the folds of our everyday lives. Thank You for the gift of Your Holy Spirit. Thank You for the opportunities You place before us to serve You and shine Your light as we serve Your children. You have given us lovely purpose right where we are today. When we shine Your light, our lives are lifted. Help us to more fully discover Your will for our lives as we study Your Word. Show us our purposes for Your kingdom. In serving You, may we find encouragement, joy, and lift. In doing so, may we connect others to Your mercy and message of salvation. To You be all honor and glory, in the name of Jesus, who is the light of the world. Amen.

ACKNOWLEDGMENTS

First and foremost, I thank my heavenly Father for making this long-held dream come true. To You be all praise and glory!

During the pandemic, my lifelong dream of writing a book got serious. I didn't want to be sitting in my wheelchair later in life, saying, "I could have written a good book but never really tried."

Asking the Lord's will and leading, my hopeful journey to authorship began with an excellent book: *The Poets & Writers Complete Guide to Being a Writer: Everything You Need to Know about Craft, Inspiration, Agents, Editors, Publishing, and the Business of Building a Sustainable Writing Career* (New York: Avid Reader Press, 2020). My grateful thanks to authors Kevin Larimer and Mary Gannon; you have done a tremendous service to aspiring writers everywhere!

Following the guidance of this book connected me to the Yates & Yates Literary Agency. I was thrilled to be accepted into their game-changing program: Author Coaching University. Many thanks to Sealy Yates, Curtis and Karen Yates, Matt Yates, and Mike Salisbury for their instruction, wisdom, and spiritual encouragement. Your training was just the boost I needed!

Thanks to our "Called to Write" writing group that grew from that program: Mark, Julie, Sandy, Casey, and Kelli. What a blessing to walk this journey with you! You have supported and prayed for me throughout this process. In moments of doubt, you encouraged me forward. Thank you and bless you!

Special thanks to my friend and talented colleague Laura Pulliam. From the beginning, your skilled help and kindness lifted my writing. Thank you for the beautiful website and the many, many ways you have helped me in this journey. I thank God for you!

To my mentor and friend Donna Snow, thank you for your generous support and encouragement. You have helped me in countless ways. God is using you so powerfully in your speaking and Bible-teaching ministry. For your kindnesses to me, hugs and gratitude always!

It's an honor to work with the team at Concordia Publishing House. Thank you for your spiritual leadership and publishing excellence. Deepest thanks to my editor, Peggy Kuethe, whose kindly expertise encouraged me spiritually and professionally from start to finish, always helping me to do my best for the Lord. It is a delight to work with you. To the array of talent across departments, thanks to each of you for your gracious and skilled help. I love walking with you and working with you on this author journey!

To Brooke Martinez, many thanks for your partnership, always in my corner with your excellent counsel and prayer support. I am grateful for you!

Special people have helped me as early readers, advisers, and loving encouragers: Meg, Michelle, Kirby, Katy, Rebecca, Diane, Eunice, Nancy, Polly, Ursula, Beth, Jamie, and others. Thanks to my neighbor friends for their sweet support: Janet, Mercedes, Michelle, Bunny, and Susan. Thank you to my church family at St. Peter: in your unique, beautiful way, you have provided a loving home base for me. Other kind souls have provided support in person and through social media—thank you, thank you!

And to my launch team: each one of you is awesome. Thank you for helping launch my book with such delight and enthusiasm. I'm grateful for your support!

My loving family: Palmer and Loribeth, Anna and Noah, Marie and Leo—for your loving kindness, listening ears, and encouragement in my writing, thank you for always rooting for me. Matt, Paul, Trish, Susie, and Tom, I'm grateful for your ongoing, gracious support. Mom, you have always encouraged my love of reading and writing; thank you. Thanks to all for your prayers and inspirational acts of kindness to others. To my ancestors, I'm grateful for your beautiful legacy of faith and service.

Love and deepest thanks to my husband, Raymond, for his steadfast belief in my writing career, his theological support, and the honor of serving beside him in ministry.

To my dearest Jesus, I see Your gentle and specific leading in every step of this journey. Thank You for trusting me with Your loving message of hope and purpose. Thank You for guiding, supporting, and protecting me. Thank You for Your mercy, leading me to this service in Your name and by Your Spirit. I'm looking to You to lead me each and every day, in every word and action. You are my light and my salvation!

Finally, dear reader, thank you for walking with me. What a privilege! I'm honored to serve beside you, sharing the love of the Lord in our small but important words and actions. May our lives be filled with God's purposes and extraordinary grace!

Soli Deo Gloria